Amazing Animal Actors

AMAZING ANIMAL ACTORS

Pauline Bartel

To Carolyn - with all good wishes!

Pauline Bartel

TAYLOR PUBLISHING
DALLAS, TEXAS

Also by Pauline Bartel:

The Complete Gone with the Wind Trivia Book

Reel Elvis!

To all the movie and television animals who brought joy to me through the years;
to my nephew, Justin Douglas Bartel, and to my niece, Erica Christine Bartel,
who give me joy today. God bless the beasts and the children.

Published by Taylor Publishing Company
1550 West Mockingbird Lane
Dallas, Texas 75235

Designed by David Timmons

Library of Congress Cataloging-in-Publication Data
Bartel, Pauline C.
    Amazing animal actors / Pauline Bartel.
      p.   cm.
    Includes bibliographical references.
    ISBN 0-87833-974-4 (pb)
    1. Animals in motion pictures. 2. Animals in television.
   I. Title.
PN1995.9.A5B37 1997
791.43'662—dc21   97-25460
                                    CIP

Printed in the United States of America
10 9 8 7 6 5 4 3 2 1

CONTENTS

ACKNOWLEDGMENTS

I would like to thank the following individuals for their love, friendship, and support during the writing of this book: my mother, Mary Bartel, my biggest fan, greatest supporter, and ablest assistant; John Boncheff, for helping a damsel in video distress; Terry Brown; Karen DeMartino; Mary Ellen Dugrenier; George, who has the strength of a lion and the gentleness of a kitten; Jennifer Jones; Sheila Levine, my attorney; Andrea Lucas; Katharine MacGregor; Joanne McFadden; Holly McGuire, my wonderful editor; members of the Arnold Madison Writers Group (Joyce Bouyea, David Lee Drotar, Jackie Craven, Kate Kunz, Peg Lewis, Jane Streiff, Donna Tomb); Carol and Alice Michon; Susan Milstrey Wells; Jan Nardolillo, who helped me to believe that anything is possible with a cup of Earl Grey tea and an occasional lunch at the Crossgates; Ellen and Dennis Navin; Dr. Frank Robinson, chiropractor extraordinaire; the Study Buddies at The College of Saint Rose (Jean Barnoski, Susan Mayer, and Kris Smith); Lynne Van Derhoof; David Van Slyke; Helen Volk; the staff at the Waterford Public Library.

To the trainers, stars, and all-around terrific people who gave their time generously, provided their special expertise, and went the extra mile to lend assistance, I give each of you a standing ovation: the Adriance Memorial Library; Eddie Albert; the American Humane Association; Joe Camp of Jungle Exotics; Bruce Campbell; MariaKay Chakas and The Lippin Group; Susan Elsner Furman of Lyrick Studios; Dennis Grisco of Grisco's Animals; Diane Hammond of the Oregon Coast Aquarium; Whitey Hughes; Frank Inn; Sassie Joiris; Shirley Jones; Jackie Kaptan; Ernie Karpels; Benay Karp of Benay's Bird and Animal Rentals; Tammy Maples of Jungle Exotics; Middletown Thrall Library; Karl Lewis Miller of Animal Action; Boone Narr of Boone's Animals for Hollywood; Clint Rowe of Animals Inc.; Kristin C. Sabo; Cheryl Shawver of Animal Actors of Hollywood; Sherel Wingard-Spencer.

Introduction

Motion picture and television animal actors have brought tears, smiles, and joy to me since I was first introduced to animal action in the 1957 film *Old Yeller*. I cried when young Travis Coates was forced to shoot the family's beloved yellow dog. But later that same day I smiled, watching television's Lassie rescue Timmy from yet another adventure. I remember my mother telling me to "wave to Lassie" as the ending credits rolled, and the collie lifted her paw as if to say, "So long! See you next week!"

Animal actors embroidered themselves into the fabric of my life with their gentleness, spirit, and courage. In the recesses of my memory, I can still hear Sergeant William Preston of the Northwest Canadian Mounted Police yell to his giant malamute Yukon King and the team of sled dogs: "On, King! On, you huskies!" I hear "Yo ho, Rinty!" echo through Fort Apache, and I see Rin Tin Tin answering the call of Rusty or Lt. Rip Masters. I get goose bumps when I recall the opening bars of Rossini's *William Tell Overture*, and the words, "A fiery horse with the speed of light, a cloud of dust and a hearty Hi-Yo, Silver. Awa-a-ay!" I know that the Lone Ranger and Silver are riding the plains, righting wrongs and helping those who need them most.

I have memories of Flicka, Fury, Trigger, and even Mr. Ed trotting through television series of the '50s and '60s and prominent pooches such as Pete the Pup, Toto, and Benji gamboling through motion pictures. I enjoyed the antics of Arnold the pig, Morris the cat, Fred the cockatoo, Flipper, Cheetah, and Gentle Ben. And my affinity for animal actors extends to those who lead the pack today: Babe, Marcel, Murray, Eddie, Wishbone, Salty, and Willy.

Amazing Animal Actors is my tribute to those four-footed, two-footed, and flippered and finned animal actors and their trainers who have amused, astounded, and entertained millions of fans from the 1920s through the 1990s. You'll find the inside scoop about the animals' training, their tricks and stunts, and all the behind-the-scenes stories about their roles in motion pictures and in television series.

Amazing Animal Actors is divided into two main sections. The first section contains in-depth profiles of forty famous animal actors, while the second section, called "Miscellaneous Menagerie," briefly spotlights more than sixty other showbiz critters who have found a home in the heart of American popular culture. You'll find each animal star listed by character name.

I also share information about those animal stars who are PATSY Award winners. Bestowed by the American Humane Association, the PATSY (Performing Animal Top Stars of the Year) is the animal equivalent of the Academy Award. The PATSY Award was established in 1951 to recognize those animal actors giving outstanding performances in motion pictures, TV, and commercials. Much like the presentation of the Oscars, the PATSY Awards were gala, yearly events from 1951 to 1986. (No PATSYs were awarded from 1979 to 1982.) Which of your favorite animal actors have PATSY Awards gracing their mantles? Turn the page to find out that and much more about *Amazing Animal Actors*.

AMAZING ANIMAL ACTORS

ARNOLD

Real Name: Arnold

Species: Chester White pig

Star Qualities: Humility. Although Arnold's amazing performances earned him industry recognition and thousands of fan letters, he remained content with perfecting the craft of acting and with accepting the occasional dog biscuit for a job well done.

Special Tricks: Arnold was famous for carrying objects (such as a lunchbox, newspaper, toys, and schoolbooks) by mouth; raiding the refrigerator by opening the door and taking out food; turning a television set on and off; "drinking" through a straw; pulling a wagon; sitting like a dog; scratching at a door; and using a pea shooter.

Most Famous Role: Arnold Ziffel in the television series *Green Acres* (CBS, 1965–1971)

Arnold shows off his piano-playing abilities to trainer Frank Inn. (*Courtesy of Frank Inn*)

Story Line

Manhattan attorney Oliver Wendell Douglas believes that being a farmer is the ideal life for him. He purchases, sight-unseen, a 160-acre farm in Hooterville from Eustace Haney, a conniving salesman of dubious goods. The farm is a nightmare of fallow fields and a shabby, unfurnished house needing major repairs. When they arrive at the farm, Oliver's sophisticated socialite wife, Lisa, is horrified at the conditions and wants to return to their New York City penthouse apartment, but Oliver convinces her to stay so he can live his Green Acres dream. The episodes chronicled their misadventures in coping with the trials and tribulations of country life and with the local zanies.

Cast

Eddie Albert . . . . Oliver Wendell Douglas
Eva Gabor . . . . Lisa Douglas

Pat Buttram..Eustace Haney
Tom Lester...Eb Dawson
Alvy Moore..Hank Kimball
Hank Patterson ....Fred Ziffel
Barbara Pepper (1965–1969) ....Doris Ziffel
Fran Ryan (1969–1970) ....Doris Ziffel
Frank Cady..Sam Drucker
Kay E. Kuter......................................Newt Kiley
Sid Melton..Alf Monroe
Mary Grace Canfield...............................Ralph Monroe
Arnold..Arnold

Adventures Behind the Scenes

Trainer Frank Inn was contacted by the television production company to provide a trained pig for the series *Green Acres.* In the series, one of Oliver and Lisa Douglas' neighbors is pig farmer Fred Ziffel. Fred has a clever pet pig named Arnold who is so smart that Fred and his wife Doris treat him as their "son." The studio wanted Inn to train a pig to be a baby in a baby carriage. Inn said, "I went out, and I got a pig, and I wrestled him until finally he would lay still, nurse on a bottle, and eat food out of my hands." Inn effected the baby-buggy pose by tying the pig's feet together and covering him with a blanket. "It took a bit of doing to keep him from squealing," Inn remembered. The production team liked the trick, used it in an episode, but didn't write any additional pig sequences into the storyline. By the time Inn received a call-back for the pig, the porker had grown to more than 300 pounds, was no longer cute, and had to be replaced.

Inn located a pig farmer with a newborn litter of pigs. Inn acquired two of the pigs and trained them to drink from a bottle and follow him around. These pigs became Arnold II. A number of other pigs played the role of Arnold during the years of the series. Inn used the pigs when they weighed 50 pounds and retired them to a breeding farm or gave them away as pets when they reached 200 pounds. The breeding farm provided subsequent Arnolds for the show.

One of Arnold's favorite food rewards was a dog biscuit that Inn and the other trainers were happy to provide. "All the trainers got along with Arnold, and they got an incredible amount of work out of him," Inn said. One of the trainers who worked with Arnold was Karl Lewis Miller, who gained subsequent fame as the provider of animal action on the movie *Babe.* According to Inn, Miller taught Arnold to do a toss, and through the magic of television, it appeared as if the newspaper that Arnold tossed flew through the air and hit the front door of the house.

Another magic-of-television trick was Arnold drinking through a straw. In reality, he just put his mouth around the straw. The liquid was then emptied from the bottom of the glass.

As Arnold's popularity increased, the stars of *Green Acres* found themselves playing second fiddle to a porker. Eddie Albert, commenting on the public's reaction to him off-screen, said: "[To them], I'm not Eddie Albert. I'm that fellow on television with the pig."

Eva Gabor remarked: "Nobody cares if I've powdered my nose. When the pig is ready, we shoot."

Inn remembered an incident that did not endear Arnold to Miss Gabor. "She received a lot of fan mail," Inn said. "One day she had about 40 fan letters, and Arnold received a fan letter. She thought it was just the cutest thing. Then she received another bunch, and Arnold received four fan letters." During this time, Inn and Arnold went on the road, promoting *Green Acres* and Arnold's celebrity status at 4-H Club shows all over the country. Many 4-H Club participants who raised pigs started Arnold fan clubs and wrote to the porcine star. "One day the postman came into the studio with three mail sacks full of letters," Inn recalled. "He dumped this bunch right on the floor and said 'Here is the fan mail!'" Gabor was there, and Inn recalled her saying, "Oh my goodness! How could I get so much fan mail?" "It's not yours," the postman replied, "These are Arnold's. Here are yours." He handed her 30 letters while Arnold had received 30,000 letters. Inn heard Gabor mutter "That dreadful pig" as she stormed off to her dressing room.

Notable Tidbits

Arnold's celebrity status earned him guest appearances on the television quiz show *What's My Line*, where he appeared as a mystery guest; and on *The Tonight Show* with Johnny Carson, where he appeared with Eva Gabor. This latter appearance created further ill will between Gabor and Arnold. Attired in a floor-length designer gown, Gabor was welcomed on stage by Carson. She took her seat in the guest chair and arranged the train of her gown to flow down the chair and onto the floor. Young, nervous Arnold was introduced and sat on the floor next to Gabor on the train of her dress. According to Inn, during the conversation with Carson, Gabor happened to look down at Arnold and found the pig relieving itself. Gabor exclaimed "Arnold, what are you doing on my dress?" According to Inn, "That told everybody what was happening. If she would have kept still, no one in the audience or on the set would have known it. The pig was sitting there and just had to go, and that was it." Carson cracked up, but Gabor was none too pleased.

Arnold was a four-time PATSY (Performing Animal Top Stars of the Year) Award winner. In 1967, Arnold placed third; in 1968, 1969, and 1971 he placed first.

Real Name: Skippy
Breed: Wire-haired terrier
Star Qualities: Aloofness. Skippy was not permitted to play with stars William Powell and
    Myrna Loy on the set of *The Thin Man* because his trainer, Henry East, feared that
    camaraderie would break the dog's concentration when the cameras rolled.
Special Tricks: Skippy ran, jumped, retrieved, and would do just about anything for a little

squeaky mouse. As Myrna Loy recalled, "I'd squeak the mouse and put it in my pocket, and then Asta would do whatever he was supposed to do because he thought he was going to get the mouse. He never got the mouse; he'd get a cracker or something."

Most Notable Role: Asta in the movie *The Thin Man* (MGM, 1934)

Plot

Nick and Nora Charles investigate the death of an inventor. The mystery is solved with the help of their clue-sniffing canine, Asta.

Cast

William Powell	Nick Charles
Myrna Loy	Nora Charles
Maureen O'Sullivan	Dorothy Wynant
Nat Pendleton	Lieutenant John Guild
Minna Gombell	Mimi Wynant
Cesar Romero	Chris Jorgenson
Natalie Moorhead	Julia Wolf
Edward Ellis	Clyde Wynant
Porter Hall	McCauley
Henry Wadsworth	Tommy
William Henry	Gilbert Wynant
Harold Huber	Nunheim
Edward Brophy	Joe Morelli
Skippy	Asta

Adventures Behind the Scenes

MGM bought the rights to a Dashiell Hammett novel, *The Thin Man*, for $14,000. In the novel, Hammett describes Asta as "a Schnauzer and not a cross between a Scottie and an Irish terrier."

Director W.S. "Woody" Van Dyke wanted to add a twist of charm, sophistication, and wit to the story of Nick and Nora Charles. Having worked with both William Powell and Myrna Loy in *Manhattan Melodrama* (MGM, 1934), Van Dyke had witnessed their on-screen professionalism as well as their off-screen camaraderie and thought they would be perfect for the roles. Studio head Louis B. Mayer worried that Powell was too old to play Nick Charles and that Loy lacked the sex appeal of Nora Charles. Van Dyke stood his ground against the studio boss and fought for a pairing that became one of the most famous husband-and-wife teams in movie history. As Asta, Skippy became their adorably funny pet with a flair for mysteries.

According to trainer Frank Inn, Skippy was owned by a special-effects man at MGM. At the time, animals were considered live props, so the property man, Henry East, rented Skippy from his owner for use in *The Thin Man*.

A fun-loving trio: Nora, Asta, and Nick Charles in *The Thin Man*.

One day on the set, East had difficulty getting Skippy to perform a trick. Frank Inn, then a janitor pushing a broom on the set, observed a frustrated East working with the recalcitrant dog. Inn told East that he knew a better way to get the dog to do the trick. East didn't believe him and asked him to demonstrate. The only experience Inn had had with dog training was with a small dog he trained as a hobby while recuperating from an automobile accident. Inn worked with Skippy, got him to do the trick, and East hired Inn on the spot as a training assistant.

Asta's first appearance in *The Thin Man* occurs at the beginning of the film. Nick Charles holds court at a swanky bar, instructing the bartender on the correct way to make a dry martini. Nora Charles strolls into the establishment carrying a tower of holiday packages and leading Asta on a leash. The terrier catches sight of Nick and scampers to greet him, sending Nora and her parcels sprawling across the floor. In directing this hilarious entrance, Van Dyke instructed Loy on how to take a fall by tripping herself. Van Dyke had the camera placed on the floor, showed Loy the mark where she was to land, and did the shot in one take with no rehearsal. According to Loy, "I must have been crazy. I could have killed myself, but my dance training paid off. I dashed in with Asta and all those packages, tripped myself, went down, slid across the floor, and hit the mark with my chin. It was absolutely incredible."

The Thin Man had a short shooting schedule of just fourteen days, so Skippy was kept busy in the Asta role. The film was a major commercial success for MGM with a first-run gross of more than $2 million.

Skippy perplexes Cary Grant and Katharine Hepburn in *Bringing Up Baby. (Museum of Modern Art/Film Stills Archive)*

Memorable Movie Moment

Under cover of darkness, Nick Charles takes Asta to Clyde Wynant's shop to search for clues to the inventor's disappearance. While in the office, Nick and Asta are startled by the arrival of Wynant's bookkeeper. "Don't make a move or that dog will tear you to shreds," Nick warns the startled man. To Nick's dismay, Asta promptly hides under a table, staying there until the action is over.

Notable Tidbits

Prior to Skippy's debut, most industry people thought that wire-haired terriers were impossible to train for movie work. According to Asta's trainer, Henry East, wire-haired terriers are "very feisty. They fight every dog, chase every cat, do everything you don't want 'em to, and don't do what you want 'em to do when you want 'em to do it." But East proved the industry wrong, and Skippy became the first wire-haired terrier to be trained for the movies.

Skippy was one photogenic pooch. His expressive, black-rimmed eyes were perfect for the silver screen because they were distinctive and did not require much makeup. His white-and-brown coat photographed well in black and white.

After renting Skippy for the first and second *Thin Man* films, East acquired a dog of his own—that he named Asta—to use in the film series. In addition to East, two other trainers—Rudd Weatherwax and Frank Inn—worked with this and other Astas who completed the sequels *After the Thin Man* (MGM, 1936); *Another Thin Man* (MGM, 1939); *Shadow of the Thin Man* (MGM, 1941); *The Thin Man Goes Home* (MGM, 1945); *Song of the Thin Man* (MGM, 1947).

Skippy later appeared with Cary Grant and Katharine Hepburn in the 1938 slapstick comedy, *Bringing Up Baby*. In that film, Skippy played a bone-burying, mischievous dog named George. The part required Skippy to "leer nastily," and Skippy was a quick study. While Skippy sat in front of a mirror, Henry East commanded "Leer!" then lifted the dog's lips to form that expression. Skippy had the look down pat in only two days.

Skippy pulled down big bucks in the acting biz. While most canine actors eked out a living at $3.50 a day, Skippy earned $250 per week.

The Thin Man films spawned a radio series called *The Adventures of the Thin Man*, which was broadcast from July 2, 1941 through September 1, 1950. Asta's mistress was played by actress Claudia Morgan, and his master was played initially by Les Damon and then at various times throughout the series by David Gothard, Les Tremayne, and Joseph Curtin. Asta was played by several dogs throughout the time the series was on the air.

Asta even made it to television. *The Thin Man* television series ran on NBC from 1957 to 1959. Peter Lawford and Phyllis Kirk played Nick and Nora Charles, and the role of Asta was played by a wire-haired terrier named Asta. This Asta won a PATSY Award in 1959 and 1960. In 1975, a ninety-minute special, *Nick and Nora*, was broadcast on ABC television, starring Craig Stevens, Jo Ann Pflug, and, of course, a dog named Asta—played by Scruffy, who had starred in the television series, *The Ghost and Mrs. Muir*.

BABE

Real Name: Babe

Breed: Large white Yorkshire pig

Star Qualities: Ad libbing. Babe proved he could ham it up with the best of them. During a scene when the porker pokes his head into a rooster house and the cockmeister orders him out, Babe deviated from the script. Rather than make a graceful exit, he executed a pratfall off the plank and onto the ground. Director Chris Noonan reshot the scene four more times, and Babe completed the scene as written in the script. But the take with the extemporaneous stunt was so funny that it was used in the film.

Special Tricks: Retrieving a metal alarm clock. Although most tricks took three or four days of training, the stealing-the-clock scene required a full ten weeks, according to animal trainer Karl Lewis Miller. The scene's multiple action sequence included Babe entering the Hoggett house, getting his rear foot tangled in yarn, grabbing the clock with his mouth, and walking down the stairs.

Most Notable Role: Babe in the film *Babe* (Universal Pictures, 1995)

Plot

Babe the talking pig defies his barnyard destiny by daring to be a sheep dog on the Hoggett farm. He learns that dreams do come true and that kindness towards others—especially sheep—makes the path of life less rocky for everyone.

Cast

Christine Cavanaugh	Voice of Babe
James Cromwell	Farmer Arthur Hoggett
Magda Szubanski	Esme Hoggett
Miriam Margolyes	Voice of Fly, the Border Collie
Danny Mann	Voice of Ferdinand, the Indian Runner Duck
Hugo Weaving	Voice of Rex, the Border Collie
Miriam Flynn	Voice of Maa, the Border Leicester Sheep
Evelyn Krape	Voice of Old Ewe, the Border Leicester Sheep
Russie Taylor	Voice of Duchess, the Blue Persian Cat
Roscoe Lee Browne	Narrator
Babe	Babe

Adventures Behind the Scenes

Babe, the novel (originally titled *The Sheep-Pig* in Britain), first came to the attention of producer George Miller while he was on a plane listening to an audio review of the book by renowned British author Dick King-Smith. Miller, who found himself laughing along with the critic over the antics of the book's animals, purchased a copy of the children's novel and

(*Archive Photos/Carolyn Jones/fotos international*)

subsequently bought the film rights. "I love the story," Miller said, "as much for its subtext as for its surface plot. It's about prejudice on a farm where each animal has his preordained place. Into this biased world comes a pig with an unprejudiced heart who takes all other creatures at face value, and by treating the sheep and all the other animals as equals, he irrevocably changes their lives and becomes world champion sheep dog in the process." Miller and director Chris Noonan wrote the screenplay for *Babe*.

The Southern Highlands, a lush green area of rolling hills 80 miles south of Sydney, Australia, and the town of Robertson were chosen as the locations for filming. The Kennedy Miller production company developed and landscaped the rented acreage with roads; gas, electric, and water facilities; two giant sheds and corrals for the animals; and a fairy-tale-type farm house and barn for the Hoggett homestead.

Animal trainer Karl Lewis Miller "loved the script" and agreed to work on *Babe* because "it was an impossible project, which meant it had my name on it." Miller supervised 56 assistants, mostly Australian agricultural students or farm workers, to train and handle the 970 animals used in the film.

The role of Babe was shared by 48 large white Yorkshire pigs. Because pigs grow quickly, 4-week-old shoats were trained in groups of six so they could begin filming when they were 15 to 17 weeks old. "Every three weeks, we'd start a new group so they'd be prepared when the preceding group outgrew its usefulness," Karl Lewis Miller said. The trainers bonded with their brood for two weeks, hand raising them with attention, love, and bottle feedings. Obedience to commands was rewarded with a click sound and a solid-food treat. All of the pigs underwent basic obedience training and then advanced training in specific stunts. The trainers had their work cut out for them. According to Miller, "I told them not to discipline the pigs because they would sulk and not to baby them as they would become too happy and giggle."

One of Babe's distinguishing physical characteristics was the small tuft of dark hair on his forehead. In reality, this hair was a toupee, and hair-and-make-up artist Carolyn Tyrer glued six hair pieces on six squealing piglets every day. Babe's normally white eyelashes were dyed black to reveal his beautiful eyes. "Everything we did had to be done in multiples as the animals had to be interchangeable," Tyrer said. "For Babe it was six, four for Fly, four for Rex, four for Maa, four for Ole Ewe, two for the horse, and up to 16 for Ferdinand. Thank heaven Whiskey the cow was perfect."

Babe proved he was a musical pig when he burst into song singing "La-la-la. La-la-la." According to trainer Karl Lewis Miller, this was excess footage of Babe sniffing the air trying to determine where the sound of sheep was coming from. Producer George Miller thought the footage charming and wanted to use it somewhere in the film. Christine Cavanaugh, the voice of Babe, mentioned that it appeared as if Babe were singing. She suggested using the song "Jingle Bells" to tie in with the Christmas segment. Producer Miller loved the idea, the footage was incorporated, and audiences chuckled to see such a multitalented pig.

Henson's Creature Shop in London and John Cox's Creature Workshop in Queensland, Australia, created animatronic clones for the lead animal actors. Computer artists created remote-controlled standing versions of the thespians, while puppeteers created sitting-and-lying-down puppet versions.

Animal dialogue comprises 80 percent of the soundtrack. The puppeteers used production audiotapes, programmed by computer into the animatronic clones, to synchronize tongue, lip, jaw, and facial movements with the dialogue.

Different animals were trained to react to different sounds. Pigs obeyed a click; ducks responded to a buzzer; dogs listened to their master's voice; and sheep reacted to a pennywhistle. New Zealand sheep trainer Caroline Girdlestone choreographed the film's finale—Babe's successful herding of sheep into a pen—with a pennywhistle clenched between her teeth, a poncho that she wielded with matador-like flourishes, and a pellet-filled tin can that she shook to gain her flock's attention. According to director Noonan, "It took a frustrating while, but eventually each animal knew his sound and responded properly. But at the start, we had some memorable traffic jams."

James Cromwell as Farmer Hoggett worked well with the animal actors. According to trainer Karl Lewis Miller, "Jamie is just natural with animals. He was always willing to bend to our needs to get the animals to perform in his presence. His pockets were filled with food and many's the time, just before or after a shot, he was willing to have a pig's sloppy mouth eat out of his hand, knowing that reward could make a big difference with the animal's performance."

For Cromwell, best known as Archie Bunker's buddy Stretch Cunningham on television's *All in the Family*, his favorite moment in *Babe* was watching the serious sheepherder-swine round up the sheep in the competition and telling him "That'll do, pig. That'll do."

Memorable Movie Moment

Farmer Hoggett wins a little pig in the guess-the-weight contest at the country fair, brings him home, and places him in the barn. Excited by the newcomer, Fly's litter of puppies questions her about what it is. She tells them that the animal is a pig, a stupid animal that the farmer and his wife will eventually eat.

The dogs scamper into the barn to investigate the new arrival and agree that the pig looks stupid. Fly comments that although pigs are smarter than sheep, pigs are still undoubtedly stupid. The little pig disagrees, startling Fly, who asks the pig's name.

"I don't know," the pig replies.

"Well, what did your mother call you to tell you apart from your brothers and sisters?"

"My mom called us all the same."

"And what was that, dear?"

"She . . . she called us all Babe."

The horse interrupts the conversation. "Perhaps we shouldn't talk too much about . . . family."

Feeling all alone and frightened, the little pig sadly lowers his head and whimpers, "I want my Mom."

Notable Tidbits

Made for a modest $25 million, *Babe* opened in August 1995 and brought home the bacon by grossing $53.7 million for the year. Even more astonishing, the film earned seven Academy Award nominations, winning an Oscar for Achievement in Visual Effects.

Babe was honored by the magazine *Entertainment Weekly* as one of its ten rookies of the year in 1995. Babe made the cut at Number Ten because, as the magazine noted, "Fame be-hooves him."

Real Name: Kris

Breed: St. Bernard

Star Qualities: Kris is a trouper. According to trainer Karl Lewis Miller, Kris performed about 99 percent of the animal action in *Beethoven*. Two other dogs were used only as lighting and rehearsal dogs.

Special Tricks: Kris can share an ice cream cone and grab a cookie from a plate. He can faint on cue, leap fences, jump through open windows, and dive into a swimming pool.

Most Famous Role: Beethoven in the movie *Beethoven* (Universal Pictures, 1992)

Plot

Despite the objections of the man of the house, a family adopts a runaway puppy that grows into a slobbering St. Bernard. The dog wins the attention of the cute guy at school for the elder daughter, saves the younger daughter from drowning, and rescues the son from bullies, but remains the bane of their dad's existence. When Beethoven falls prey to an unscrupulous veterinarian, Dad comes to the rescue, saves the dog, and blows the lid off a city-wide dognapping operation.

Cast

Charles Grodin	George Newton
Bonnie Hunt	Alice Newton
Dean Jones	Doctor Herman Varnick
Nicolle Tom	Ryce
Christopher Castile	Ted
Sarah Rose Karr	Emily
Oliver Platt	Harvey
Stanley Tucci	Vernon
David Duchovny	Brad
Patricia Heaton	Brie
Kris	Beethoven

Adventures Behind the Scenes

Animal trainer Karl Lewis Miller acquired 12 dogs and trained them for 24 weeks to fill the role of Beethoven. Kris was the second dog acquired, and Miller knew that the six-month-old pup from a breeding kennel in Riverside, California, was special. "Kris had all the natural personality traits and instincts of the written character Beethoven," Miller said. "Everything we taught him to do he did in such a manner that in our minds we saw Beethoven above and beyond the other dogs that were in training." Kris was chosen as the main dog for the film.

According to Miller, the script contained good dog action. During the first days of shooting, however, the producer and director were concerned because Kris performed the tricks but not with the flavor that they had imagined. "I explained to them that a St. Bernard's anatomy does not allow him to be as graceful as most other breed dogs," Miller said. "He will jump in and save the girl from drowning but not as gracefully as a golden retriever. He'll snarl at the bullies and save the boy from being picked on but not as viciously as a Doberman. He'll sit up and beg but not as cute as a poodle. Once they got it instilled in their minds that he was doing all the tricks as a St. Bernard would do, a star was born. Kris became Beethoven, and he has been Beethoven ever since."

When Beethoven is at the veterinarian's office for his shot, he suspiciously eyes the vet's assistant as she prepares the needle and syringe. Beethoven's eyes roll back in his head, and he faints on the exam table. According to Miller, the simulated eye rolling for this scene was accomplished using an animatronic head that was an exact replica of Kris' head.

The animatronic head was also used in the scene in which Beethoven was in bed with George Newton and rolls over to snuggle next to Dad. If Kris himself had rolled over, his legs would have stood straight up, ruining the effect of the scene. "The turnover was actually a man in a dog costume wearing the animatronic head," Miller said. That scene was a combination of Kris starting to roll over, the man turning, and Kris completing the flop and breathing hard into actor Charles Grodin's face.

Memorable Movie Moments

While trying to retrieve a ball that has strayed into the babysitter's in-ground pool, young Emily Newton falls in and struggles in the

Beethoven likes things on the cool side. (*Archive Photos/Darlene Hammond*)

deep water. Sensing danger at a distance, Beethoven unlocks the gate of his enclosure at the Newton home, runs across the yard and through the neighborhood, jumps over a fence and a backyard sunbather, crashes through bushes, and leaps into the pool. He swims underneath the drowning Emily and carries her on his back to safety.

Notable Tidbits

In addition to his work in *Beethoven*, Kris has been an atmosphere, or extra, dog in a movie-of-the-week, had a cameo role on the television series *Step By Step*, and appeared in a still ad for an automobile service.

In 1993, Kris returned to feature film work by starring in *Beethoven's 2nd* in which he finds true love with a St. Bernard named Missy and starts a family with four puppies: Chubby, Mohawk, Tchaikovsky, and Dolly. During the filming, director Rod Daniel kept the on-set temperature at a nippy 60 degrees to accommodate his bulky star. "He's a 120-pound dog. If it gets any hotter, he becomes this canine drooling machine and poops out," Daniel said. To those of his cast and crew who complained about the cold, Daniel had a recommendation: "I told them to put on a sweater."

BENJI

Real Name: Higgins
Breed: Mixed breed (part poodle, part cocker spaniel, part schnauzer)
Star Qualities: A tireless promoter. To promote *Benji*, Higgins and his trainer Frank Inn traveled by Benjimobile to more than 60 cities, making as many as eight appearances daily.
Special Tricks: Benji's most amazing ability was showing emotions through his facial expressions. His special tricks included opening a mailbox and removing a letter, yawning, and sneezing on cue.
Most Famous Role: Benji in the movie *Benji* (Mulberrry Square Productions, 1974)

Plot

A lovable stray dog befriends various people in a small town including the owner of a cafe, a police officer, a woman with a cat, and a brother and sister. When the children are kidnapped, the clever canine comes to the rescue, thwarting the kidnappers and gaining a real home.

Cast

Patsy Garrett	Mary
Allen Fiuzat	Paul
Cynthia Smith	Cindy
Peter Breck	Dr. Chapman
Frances Bavier	Lady with the Cat
Terry Carter	Officer Tuttle
Edgar Buchanan	Bill
Christopher Connelly	Henry
Deborah Walley	Linda
Mark Slade	Mitch
Tom Lester	Riley
Herburt Vigran	Lt. Samuels
Higgins	Benji

Trainer Frank Inn and Benji (Higgins) on location. (*Courtesy of Frank Inn*)

Adventures Behind the Scenes

Trainer Frank Inn found his "All-American dog" at the Burbank Animal Shelter in the early 1960s. "They were going to put him to sleep if they didn't find a home for him," Inn recalled. "So I took him to keep him from having that kind of problem." Inn named the dog Higgins, and trained him. Higgins landed a role on the television series *Petticoat Junction*, which debuted on CBS in 1963. He played the family pet of the Bradley family, proprietors of the Shady Rest Hotel in Hooterville. "The dog was absolutely terrific," Inn said. "He learned a different trick every week for 39 weeks out of the year for seven years on *Petticoat Junction*." When the series ended in 1970, Higgins was almost 14 years old, and Inn decided to allow the dog to retire.

Frank Inn with Benji and his successor in 1975. (*Courtesy of Frank Inn*)

Joe Camp, an independent film maker and president of Mulberry Square Productions in Dallas, Texas, dreamed of writing, producing, and directing a major film about a vagabond dog from the dog's perspective. In 1973, Camp visited Hollywood dog trainers and finally found the dog he wanted on his last stop, a visit to Frank Inn. Camp spied Higgins relaxing under a tree in the front yard and asked Inn what the dog could do. "'That dog can do anything, but he's old', I told him," Inn said. Camp asked if the dog could come to a window and yawn. "I picked Higgins up and tossed him up on the roof of the porch, and he turned around, and I had him sit and yawn." Camp was amazed and persuaded Inn to bring Higgins out of retirement to star in the film *Benji*.

After agreeing to do *Benji*, Inn began an exercise program for Higgins to build him up so that he could perform the tricks in the script. Inn accomplished this by riding a motorcycle around his property and having Higgins run after him.

Filming *Benji* challenged the movie makers. "It makes for interesting challenges," Camp said, "when you have to come up with new ways to do things like follow a dog running thirty-five miles per hour with the camera four feet away at his eye level." In fact, the studio had to design special support equipment for the cameras so that the lenses were positioned four inches off the ground. Traditional, standard-sized support equipment such as tripods and dollies position the camera much higher off the ground.

Frank Inn worked with Higgins through the filming, cueing the dog from behind the camera. As Inn related at the time, "Benji senses the mood that I'm in, then he develops that same mood. He can be happy or sad or angry, depending on whether I'm acting happy, sad, or angry. Benji is even happy to look sad because he knows he has pleased me."

The print ads that ran in national magazines to herald the debut of the film featured a photo of Higgins with a rascally gleam in his eye and the caption "Robert Redford, move over. America has a new most-huggable hero."

The reviews for this unusual film singled out the performance of its canine star. *Variety* wrote: "In this case it isn't a dog performing, but a dog acting, just as humans act." *The National Observer* wrote: "The film features one of the most accomplished canine actors in America. He can, it seems, do just about anything on command and even (I swear!) show emotion."

Memorable Movie Moment

Hoping to help rescue Paul and Cindy, Benji returns to the old house where they are being held hostage by the kidnappers, Mitch, Linda, Henry, and Riley. Benji creeps down the staircase and spies the "sloppy-try" version of the ransom note, crumpled on the floor. Tension is high among the kidnappers and erupts into an argument. Benji bides his time. Suddenly, Mitch spots Benji, and recognizes him as the children's dog. Benji scampers down the stairs and grabs the note. Mitch, Henry, and Riley back Benji into a corner, trying to get the note away from him. Benji makes a break for it, but Mitch catches him. Just then Benji's friend, the dainty dog Tiffany, pops out of hiding and bites Mitch's leg. Now free, Benji runs up the staircase but hesitates to leave because he sees an angry Mitch kick Tiffany. Her fallen form lies still on the floor. Henry and Riley run up the stairs after Benji, and Benji bolts. He escapes from the house and yard, runs through town and down the street to the

Benji, in his own custom space suit, tours NASA. (*Archive Photos*)

Chapman house, and slips in through the Chapman's backdoor with the copy of the ransom note clenched firmly between his teeth.

Notable Tidbits

Higgins won a PATSY Award in 1966 for his work in *Petticoat Junction*. In 1975, the American Humane Association inducted Higgins as Benji into their Hall of Fame. The only prior honoree was Lassie. The American Guild of Variety Artists bestowed upon Higgins their Georgie Award and named Higgins "Animal Act of the Year for 1976."

Joe Camp decided to film a sequel to *Benji* called *For the Love of Benji* (1977). Higgins was far too elderly to take on the strenuous part of a dog on the loose in Greece, so his daughter took on the role of *Benji* for her father. Frank Inn had named the daughter Benjean, but when she took on the role that had made her father famous, Inn called her Benji.

Benji and Benji descendants continued the Benji tradition in films such as *Oh, Heavenly Dog!* (1980), and *Benji the Hunted* (1987), and in television specials such as *The Phenomenon of Benji* (1978)—the first prime time special starring a dog—*Benji's Very Own Christmas Story* (1978), and in the series *Benji, Zax, and the Alien Prince* (1983–1984).

Real Name: Bingo
Breed: Mixed breed (part border collie, part collie)
Star Qualities: Personality. "Bingo loves to work; she loves to please. She's a quick learner," according to trainer Boone Narr of Boone's Animals for Hollywood.
Special Tricks: Bingo has 55 behaviors in her repertoire, including retrieving; picking up her front paw; grabbing her tail and spinning in a circle; sitting up and covering her eyes with her paws; waving good-bye; digging, yawning, sneezing, and jumping on command.
Most Famous Role: Bingo in the movie *Bingo* (Tri-Star Pictures, 1991)

Plot

After running away from the circus, Bingo befriends a boy whose parents will not allow him to have a dog. When the family moves from Colorado to Wisconsin, Bingo tracks the boy and along the way liberates a passel of pooches from a hot-dog maker, rescues a family from gunmen holding them hostage, and escapes from prison after being wrongly convicted for participating in an armored-car robbery. Bingo finds the boy, but before they can enjoy a happy reunion, the youngster is kidnapped. Bingo saves the boy, and the boy's parents agree that Bingo can become part of the family.

Cast

Cindy Williams . . . . Natalie Devlin
David Rasche . . . . Hal Devlin
Robert J. Steinmiller, Jr. . . . . Chuckie Devlin
David French . . . . Chickie Devlin
Kurt Fuller . . . . Lennie
Joe Guzaldo . . . . Eli
Suzie Plakson . . . . Ginger
Glenn Shadix . . . . Duke
Wayne Robson . . . . Four Eyes
Simon Webb . . . . Steve
Tamsin Kelsey . . . . Bunny
Bingo . . . . Bingo

Adventures Behind the Scenes

Director Matthew Robbins and animal trainer Boone Narr teamed up to locate a dog for the role of Bingo. The pair looked at more than 500 Hollywood dogs, but the director wasn't satisfied with any of them, so Narr continued hunting. After three months of searching, one of Narr's trainers discovered a dog at the Castaic, California animal shelter. According to Narr, "I showed Matthew pictures of the dog, and he said, 'My God, that's the dog! That's the dog I want!'"

The female dog that had been plucked from the pound for stardom was a mother with a frisky puppy. Rather than split up the family, Narr acquired both dogs from the animal shelter for the film. The puppy, named Maui, was a double for his mother in *Bingo*. "We saved the actress for her closeups, of course," Narr said.

Narr worked Bingo for six months to learn the behaviors used in the film. "It would have been nice if I had an easy dog to train," according to Narr, "but she was extremely stubborn and difficult. I got to use a lot of my training talents to really pull from a dog that was extremely hard to train. She's my favorite because she gave me so much back out of that movie." Performing with panache, Bingo carried a bucket of water, turned on a faucet, stood on hind legs while holding a ball in her mouth, rode a skateboard, walked on her hind legs along a sobriety line, attacked an armored-car thief, and licked plates clean while working as an assistant dishwasher in a greasy-spoon restaurant.

"She patterns very well," Narr said. Performing a pattern involves doing a sequence of events. For example, in the luggage factory fire scene, Bingo had to loosen the ropes binding Chuckie's hands, remove the gag from his mouth, climb up to a platform, jump to a ramp, and contemplate leaping through the fire to activate a fire alarm. "We got her to do that with no trouble at all because she knew it was a pattern. She knew to repeat the sequence," Narr said. The patterns worked especially well when multiple takes of a single scene were required. "She adapted quite well, and we tried to make it a real positive experience each time," Narr said.

Part of the positive experience for Bingo were the rewards that Narr presented to her—

a squeaky toy, a pat on the head, a verbal "good girl," or a food treat. For Narr, however, the food rewards drove him crazy. "She's an extremely finicky eater. Extremely finicky," Narr said. "She only likes certain things on certain days, so I had to pack a whole lunch box when I went to the set with her because she turns her nose up at so many things." Favorite tidbits, "depending on the day," included cooked chicken, a dog kibble, a piece of liver, or a piece of beef with garlic.

Memorable Movie Moment

While attempting a bicycle jump off a dock and across a stream, Chuckie Devlin crashes into the water and is knocked unconscious, face down in the swirling current. Bingo pulls Chuckie out of the water by his pant leg, turns him over onto his back, and unzips the boy's jacket with his teeth. Realizing that the boy isn't breathing, Bingo heads for the dock, makes a grand running leap off the platform, lands on the boy's chest in a canine version of CPR, and watches as the boy spits up water and regains consciousness.

Notable Tidbits

Although the movie *Bingo* was not a box-office success, the film on video has made its star a household name among children. Bingo especially enjoys making personal appearances. "She loves kids. She's just a ham with kids," Narr said.

Bingo has appeared in television commercials for Purina Dogchow, Ken-L Ration, and Nike; she has been an atmosphere, or extra, dog in various motion pictures.

Bingo watched her son, Maui, grow up to follow in his mother's pawprints. Maui appears as Jamie and Paul Buchman's dog, Murray, on the television series, *Mad About You*; and Bingo works on the show as Maui's backup dog.

Real Name: Peggy

Species: Chimpanzee

Star Qualities: Simpatico simian with directors. Working with Peggy as Bonzo was "a fascinating experience," according to Ronald Reagan. "The normal procedure called for the director, Fred de Cordova, to tell the trainer what he wanted from Bonzo. But time after time, Freddie, like the rest of us, was so captivated that he'd forget and start to direct Bonzo as he did the human cast members. He'd say 'No, Bonzo, in this scene you should . . .' Then he'd hit his head and cry: 'What the hell am I doing?'"

Special Tricks: Peggy could do flips in a crib, ride a tricycle, open doors, climb out windows, jump into and out of the back seat of an automobile, and remove and replace a necklace from a jewelry store.

Bonzo (Peggy) and future president Ronald Reagan.

Most Famous Role: Bonzo in the movie *Bedtime for Bonzo* (Universal, 1951)

Plot

Wishing to prove that environment rather than heredity influences behavior, professor of psychology Peter Boyd borrows a chimpanzee from the zoology department at Sheridan College and raises the chimp as his "son" with the help of a blonde nanny, Jane Linden. When the "family" breaks up, the distressed chimpanzee steals a costly necklace, but the professor is caught with the goods by the police. After the chimp is persuaded to return the necklace, Peter and Jane reunite the "family" through the bonds of holy matrimony.

Cast

Ronald Reagan	Professor Peter Boyd
Diana Lynn	Jane Linden
Walter Slezak	Professor Hans Neumann
Lucille Barkley	Valerie Tillinghast
Herbert Heyes	Dean Tillinghast
Jesse White	Babcock
Herburt Vigran	Lt. Daggett
Joel Friedkin	Mr. DeWitt
Peggy	Bonzo

Adventures Behind the Scenes

A native of Liberia, Africa, Peggy's screen debut was in the 1948 film *Jungle Jim*, starring Johnny Weissmuller, Virginia Grey, George Reeves, Lita Baron, Rick Vallin, and Holmes Herbert. Peggy played the role of Jungle Jim's faithful companion, Tamba.

The story idea for *Bedtime for Bonzo* was inspired by a real-life Yale anthropologist who in the 1940s experimented with raising a chimpanzee as a human child. Universal paid $18,000 for the script.

Peggy was valued at $50,000 and pulled down a weekly salary of up to $1,000. The chimpanzee had three movie stand-ins.

Ronald Reagan enjoyed working with Peggy but admitted that "Diana Lynn, Walter Slezak, and I fought a losing battle against a scene-stealer with a built-in edge." Peggy may have been adorable to work with, but the chimp was also unpredictable. Once on the set, Peggy grabbed Reagan's necktie and kept pulling, almost strangling the actor.

Memorable Movie Moment

Bonzo plays with the telephone, and the operator comes on the line. Bonzo makes choking sounds into the receiver, causing the operator to conclude that an emergency situation exists. The operator verifies the address of the caller then dispatches the fire and police departments to the scene. When they arrive, Bonzo's "papa" has some quick explaining to do.

Notable Tidbits

Peggy and co-star Ronald Reagan were scheduled to host the first PATSY Award ceremony in 1951. Equivalent to the Academy Award, the PATSY Award was bestowed by the American Humane Association to recognize outstanding animal performances in motion pictures, television, and commercials. Unfortunately, before Peggy could appear, a fire swept through a Quonset hut at the World Jungle Compound where Peggy and her three chimpanzee stand-ins were being housed. Although Peggy escaped the flames, she suffered from smoke inhalation. Fire personnel worked on her for 30 minutes but failed to resuscitate her.

The sequel to *Bedtime for Bonzo* was 1952's *Bonzo Goes to College*, which starred Maureen O'Sullivan, Charles Drake, Edmund Gwenn, Gigi Perreau, Gene Lockhart, Irene Ryan, David Janssen, and another chimpanzee called Bonzo II. Ronald Reagan declined to be included in the production.

During the 1980 Presidential campaign, Reagan was asked by an Associated Press reporter to autograph a movie still from *Bedtime for Bonzo* that showed Reagan and Peggy in bed. Ever apt with a one-liner and no doubt remembering his cuddly co-star, Reagan scrawled: "I'm the one with the watch."

CHAMPION

Real Name: Little Champ
Breed: Tennessee walking horse
Star Qualities: Intelligence. Champion learned quickly a large repertoire of tricks and stunts.
Special Tricks: When Champion and Gene Autry performed in live shows, their most spectacular stunt was jumping through a gigantic poster of themselves. This trick illustrated the great degree of trust that Champion had in Autry because, to the horse, the poster looked like a solid wall.
Most Famous Role: Champion in the television series *The Adventures of Champion* (CBS, 1955–1956)

Western star Gene Autry and Champion, "The World's Wonder Horse." (*Movie Star News*)

Story Line

Twelve-year-old Ricky North owns a talented horse, Champion, and a faithful German Shepherd, Rebel, and lives on a ranch owned by his Uncle Sandy. Episodes related the boy's proclivity for becoming involved in dangerous situations with natural disasters, murderers, thieves, and other troublemakers and the boy's rescues by Champion and Rebel performing unusual feats of animal derring-do.

Cast

Barry Curtis . . . . Ricky North
Jim Bannon . . . . Sandy North
Francis McDonald . . . . Will Calhoun
Ewing Mitchell . . . . Sheriff Powers
Little Champ . . . . Champion

Adventures Behind the Scenes

Between 1936 and 1954, Gene Autry made more than 70 films with his famous horse, Champion. A former equestrian director for Ringling Brothers' Circus, John Agee was Champion's trainer. Under Agee's tutelage, Champion soon became known as "the World's Wonder Horse" because it was thought that he knew more tricks and stunts than any other horse actor at the time. Champion knew how to bow, kneel; do the waltz, hula, and the Charleston; laugh; kiss; and sign his name. Agee even taught Champion a spectacular, crowd-pleasing stunt—running at full gallop and then jumping onto a specially-prepared piano while his trainer tickled the ivories.

Several horses played Champion over the years. Acquired by Autry in Oklahoma, the original horse had dark sorrel coloring with a blaze face and white stockings. Autry paid $1,500 for the second Champion—called Champion, Jr.—and according to Autry that was the highest amount he ever spent for a horse. Champion, Jr. starred in Autry's postwar films. In 1950, Autry retired Champion, Jr., and used his successor, Little Champ, for the television series. Acclaimed horse trainer Glenn Randall trained Little Champ. Each horse had a number of stand-ins. "The original Champion had four stand-ins at a time when Greta Garbo had one," Autry said.

The original Champion even had a double for live performances on stage and at rodeos. That horse was Tom Mix's second horse, Tony, Jr. After Mix's film career ended, he leased a horse named Lindy, later renamed Tony, Jr., that he used to tour with the circus. When Mix retired, Lindy's owner, John Agee, approached Autry about leasing Lindy for his in-person performances. Because Lindy also resembled Champion, Autry leased the horse and also hired Agee to train Champion.

The films led to two television series. The first, *The Gene Autry Show* was broadcast from 1950 to 1956 and featured Autry the singing cowboy, his silly sidekick Pat Buttram, and Little Champ showing off his talents. The theme song was "Back in the Saddle Again." In 1955, Little Champ starred in his own show, *The Adventures of Champion*, which was produced by Gene Autry's Flying A Productions. Director of the series Ford Beebe claimed that shooting the series was grueling. Actor Barry Curtis who played young Ricky North was often absent from the set for his school lessons, and Rebel the dog and Little Champ hated each other. Despite this personality conflict, Little Champ was compensated well for what he had to endure. He earned $2,500 per episode.

Notable Tidbits

When Champion traveled, he did it in style. He had a three-room trailer complete with piped-in music and running water. He was also the first horse to fly across the country. In 1940, Champion flew on a TWA DC-3 airplane modified to accommodate the horse and his owner on a trip from California to New York. According to Autry, "Five rows of seats were removed at the rear of the craft and a private stall created, including a metal trough with hay heaped across the bottom. A harness dangled from the ceiling, so Champion could be strapped in for safety if the weather turned rough." Whenever the plane encountered turbulence, Autry fed Champion an apple to keep his mind off the rough air.

CLARENCE

Real Name: Freddie

Species: Lion

Star Qualities: Unique look. Freddie was a cross-eyed cub almost given away because of his ocularly-challenged look. However, producer Ivan Tors felt that Freddie offered something special. "I've never seen a cross-eyed lion and neither has the rest of the world," Tors said at the time. Tors decided to turn the deficiency into an advantage, changed the lion's name to Clarence because it sounded funnier than Freddie, and made the cat a star.

Special Tricks: Clarence purred when anyone rubbed his back.

Most Famous Role: Clarence in the television series *Daktari* (CBS, 1966–1969)

Story Line

An American veterinarian and his daughter run an animal study center in Africa. Episodes related their adventures with natives, poachers, and animals, including their pets, a lion and a chimpanzee.

Cast

Marshall Thompson	Dr. Marsh Tracy
Cheryl Miller	Paula Tracy
Yale Summers	Jack Dane (1966–1968)
Hedley Mattingly	Hedley
Hari Rhodes	Mike
Ross Hagen	Bart Jason (1968–1969)

(*Archive Photos/MGM-TV*)

Erin Moran . . . . Jenny Jones
(1968–1969)
Clarence . . . . .Clarence

Adventures Behind the Scenes

As a cub, Clarence was raised with affection training at Africa, USA, an animal compound located outside of Los Angeles. The compound was run by animal trainer Ralph Helfer in partnership with film and television producer Ivan Tors of *Flipper* fame. Affection training involved allowing African and Asian wild animals to roam freely through a simulated jungle setting and encouraging daily touching and petting by the trainers. With the affection lavished upon Clarence, he grew to be a friendly, even-tempered, non-aggressive creature. Tors described him as "the Shirley Temple of the lion world."

Clarence was born cross-eyed. His trainer Ralph Helfer did not notice that the condition caused the young lion any particular problems until Clarence began his training. One day Helfer and his trainers were teaching Clarence to jump into the back of a station wagon that had its rear door down. One of the trainers hopped into the car and called to the lion. "As Clarence approached the car, the trainer enticed him with a piece of meat," Helfer said. "He eagerly ran toward the wagon, jumped up, and ran smack into the side-door frame. He fell back, a bit dizzy from his encounter, and then tried again. Again he clobbered his head on the framework." That incident brought the vet to the compound to examine Clarence. The vet thought that the vision problem might correct itself as Clarence grew older but suggested a training program to help him use his eyes properly. His training involved moving through a long walkway shaped like a funnel, which forced Clarence to focus his eyes as he made his way through it. Another similar contraption featured a center path with ditches dug on either side that caused the lion's feet to slip if he veered from walking a straight line. An ophthalmologist even suggested that Clarence wear special prescription glasses. A lion-sized pair was made, Clarence wore them, and looked silly until they proved useless and were subsequently discarded. Clarence's vision improved as the years went by.

Clarence's first foray into feature films was his starring role in *Clarence, The Cross-Eyed Lion* (1965) which was shot at Africa, USA. His human co-stars were Marshall Thompson and Cheryl Miller; animal co-stars included Doris the chimp and Mary Lou the python.

The great success of the film lead to a television series, *Daktari* (meaning "doctor" in Swahili), which followed a similar storyline. On the first day of filming, Clarence waited calmly near the set for his first scene. A production assistant armed with a clapboard called for quiet, clapped the boards together, then gave the order to "Roll it!" Startled by the sudden noise, Clarence took off like a shot. According to Tors, "He jumped 20 feet over the camera and disappeared up the mountain. It took us an hour and a half . . . to find him."

During the filming of *Daktari*, the camera occasionally shared Clarence's cross-eyed point of view with the audience by showing a scene focused in double vision.

On camera, Clarence was asked to do many unusual stunts. One involved incubating a dozen abandoned ostrich eggs. When the chicks hatched, they swarmed all over Clarence, making for a cute scene. Off camera, he indulged the hijinks of his co-star Judy the Chimp by allowing her to jump up and down on his back or pull his tail when he was asleep.

Because of his gentle nature, Clarence rarely snarled. When a snarl was needed, Clarence's trainers turned to a double lion named Leo who was kept in the animal compound. Leo looked exactly like Clarence except for the crossed eyes, but because of abuse by a prior owner, Leo was mean and vicious. In addition to snarls, Leo occasionally contributed on-camera attacks and action in long shots, but he was always under the tightest security.

Notable Tidbits

Clarence won a PATSY Award in 1966 for his work in *Clarence, The Cross-Eyed Lion* and in 1968 for his work in *Daktari*.

CLEO

Real Name: Bernadette

Breed: Pedigreed basset hound

Star Qualities: Distinctive features. Bernadette had long, beautiful ears. In fact, her ears were so long that she often stepped on them.

Special Tricks: Bernadette could lie down on her tummy with her hind legs splayed out behind her, balance a ball at the end of her nose, then crawl and bark like a seal. While blindfolded, she could climb a ladder and walk a tightwire. She could fall over backward and stand on her head in a corner and walk on her hind legs.

Most Famous Role: Cleo in the television series *The People's Choice* (CBS, 1955–1958)

Story Line

While studying to become a lawyer, Socrates "Sock" Miller, an ornithologist with the Bureau of Fish and Wildlife, is elected to the city council of New City, California. His zeal for community service sometimes puts him at odds with Mayor John Peoples who also happens to be the father of Sock's girlfriend, Mandy. Observing the action is Sock's pet basset hound, Cleo, who at pertinent moments turns to the camera and allows the audience to hear her sarcastic thoughts about the situation.

Cast

Jackie Cooper	Socrates "Sock" Miller
Patricia Breslin	Amanda "Mandy" Peoples
Paul Maxey	Mayor John Peoples
Margaret Irving	Aunt Augusta "Gus" Miller
Mary Jane Croft	Voice of Cleo
Bernadette	Cleo

Adventures Behind the Scenes

Animal trainer Frank Inn was called to Jackie Cooper's office to meet with the production team for *The People's Choice*. Cooper was familiar with Inn's work and wanted the trainer to find and train a sad-faced dog for the series. Through a contact, Inn and his partner located a basset hound for sale. "We looked at it, and it was a sad-faced basset, but it seemed rather timid," Inn said. Inn bought the dog, named Bernadette, for $85—a price that Inn regarded as cheap—and his partner put the dog in their car. After the men had complet-

On behalf of the March of Dimes, Cleo (Bernadette) displays her skills with Frank Inn before a young, awestruck audience in 1958. (*Courtesy of Frank Inn*)

ed the transaction with the seller, they returned to the car only to discover that Bernadette had pulled the car keys out of the ignition, chewed through the leather strap of the key chain, and scattered the keys all over the floor. That was Inn's first inkling that all was not quite right with the dog. Inn's partner hopped into the backseat with Bernadette. "The dog strained at the leash and got up on the back of the seat and was breathing down my neck," Inn remembered. "All of a sudden, the dog got car sick and vomited." Things were not going well.

Inn brought Bernadette to Jackie Cooper's production team, and they liked her even though she was nervous. The team gave Inn the script for the pilot and told him that they wanted to start shooting in two weeks. "There wasn't an awful lot of stuff that the dog had to do," Inn said. But Bernadette's nervousness worried Inn, and he was not sure he could train the dog in that short a period of time. However, he promised that he would try.

As a result of her nervousness, Bernadette didn't have an appetite. To gain the dog's confidence, to lessen the nervousness, and to begin the training, Inn set his alarm clock to ring every two hours. When the alarm went off, Inn played with Bernadette for about ten minutes. During those periods, Inn trained her for the behaviors required in the script: to sit, stay, lie down, bark, carry things in her mouth, pick up keys, and sit up. "I worked with her around the clock. I even went to a motel so I wouldn't be disturbed," Inn said. "After a couple of days of that round-the-clock stuff, I was up all the time." Inn trained Bernadette with food rewards, which seemed to stimulate her appetite.

Two weeks later, Inn and Bernadette reported for work on the pilot. He thought his hard work had paid off because she had learned all the tricks needed for the episode. Additionally, Bernadette's appetite had returned although she still was thin. "Well, the next thing I knew, when we were in front of the camera, the dog was camera shy," Inn said. Bernadette was even fearful when the clapboard sounded at the beginning of a take. Because Bernadette was used to Inn clapping his hands as part of her training, Inn resorted to clapping his hands instead of having the clapboard sound announce the take.

Inn was called out of town for two weeks to provide animal action on the James Dean and Elizabeth Taylor film *Giant*. In his absence, Inn instructed his wife to feed Bernadette regularly. The dog had so much confidence in Mrs. Inn that when the trainer returned he found that "that basset hound was so fat, it was as broad as it was long." And a good thing, too, that Bernadette had blossomed because Inn received word that *The People's Choice* would go into production.

Inn subsequently learned why he had been able to acquire Bernadette for such an inexpensive price. "She had been sold three times before," Inn said. "She had chewed up things in the house, the owners couldn't housebreak her, and they had all kinds of problems. But once I got her and worked with her, I had no problems. It just took a little while."

Mr. Ed may have had to move his lips to communicate, but Cleo was more sophisticated than that. Instead, she turned toward the camera and maintained a deadpan expression while the disembodied voice of actress Mary Jane Croft provided Cleo's "thoughts" and wise-cracking comments. Croft had played a former schoolmate of Lucy's in a 1954 episode of *I Love Lucy*. While *The People's Choice* was in production, Croft also had the role of Betty Ramsey, Lucy's Westport, Connecticut, neighbor on *I Love Lucy* from January 1957 to May 1957. Croft did not realize that she was supplying the voice for a dog until the first day she arrived for work at the studio; she did not meet Bernadette until after she had provided Cleo's voice for 37 episodes.

Notable Tidbits

Once Bernadette became comfortable with her stardom, she and Frank Inn went on the road for publicity appearances for the March of Dimes and Easter Seals campaigns and for personal appearances at veterans' homes and hospitals.

After *The People's Choice* series ended, Bernadette made appearances on a number of television shows, including *Ozzie and Harriet*, *The Bob Cummings Show*, *The Perry Como Show*, *The Beverly Hillbillies*, and *The Danny Thomas Show*.

Bernadette was awarded a PATSY Award in 1958. In the television category for that year, Bernadette as Cleo was the second place winner between Lassie in first place and Rin Tin Tin in third place.

COMET

Real Name: Comet

Breed: Golden Retriever

Star Qualities: Craves attention. He becomes upset and pouts if he doesn't get his trainer's full attention.

Special Tricks: Comet shows great versatility by being able to do a convincing leg attack and by being able to blow out a birthday-cake candle. Additionally, he can sit up; roll over on his back; stretch; crawl; raise one paw; catch his tail; walk on his hind legs; put a hot dog on his nose, flip it, and then catch it; howl; yawn; scratch a flea; shake hands; snarl; and leap into the air.

Most Famous Role: Comet in the television series *Full House* (ABC, debuted 1987)

Story Line

After the death of his wife in an automobile accident, a sportscaster turned talk-show host joins forces with his brother-in-law and his best friend to raise three young daughters. Episodes related the escapades of an unconventional family, coping with the ups and downs of life and love.

Cast

Bob Saget	Danny Tanner
John Stamos	Jesse Katsopolis
Dave Coulier	Joey Gladstone
Candace Cameron	D.J. Tanner
Jodie Sweetin	Stephanie Tanner
Mary Kate and Ashley Fuller Olsen	Michelle Tanner
Lori Loughlin	Rebecca Donaldson-Katsopolis
Benji and Kevin Wilhoit	Nicky and Alex Katsopolis
Comet	Comet

Adventures Behind the Scenes

According to Cheryl Shawver of Animal Actors of Hollywood, Comet was found through a golden retriever rescue. (A rescue organization's members scout animal shelters for a particular breed of dog and then match those dogs to willing owners.) "He had been turned in by a family that said he was impossible to live with," Shawver said. "They said he was nuts, not mean, but that he just chewed up everything he touched. All that energy that they hated, we channeled into training, and he became a genius."

The production team for *Full House* sought a dog to portray a female having puppies, and Comet was selected for the role. A few subsequent episodes included the puppies, and the reaction from the audience was so positive that the storyline was changed to include keeping one of the puppies as a family pet. The production team selected Comet for the role of the family dog, and because they liked the animal actor's name, they decided to use Comet as the name for the character dog.

As lead dog on the series, Comet used his boundless energy to learn tricks and stunts quickly and to become an expert at patterning. A pattern involves a complicated series of tricks such as entering a room, going to a table, picking up an object, bringing the object to another place, and then curling up to take a snooze. He didn't mind endless retakes. In fact, according to Shawver, most animals poop out after a few takes, but Comet could do 20 and be as fresh as if he were only just getting started.

Trainers motivated Comet with toys of all kinds. "Anything that he can play with, he loves," Shawver said. "He'd play with a stick. If there's nothing else, a rock. He just loves to play." His favorite food motivators include liver, garlic, and stew beef.

Notable Tidbits

"Comet loves to have things to do, to think about things, and all that great energy is wonderful for us to work with," Shawver said. Although Comet does most of the animal action, he has a double named Ajax. "He can do as much as Comet can. He's qualified in his own right to be a lead dog," Shawver said. In fact, Ajax is lead dog on *The Drew Carey Show* (ABC).

Shawver calls Comet a very special dog. "With the knowledge he has and with his intelligence to understand what they're trying to show him, his trainers feel comfortable when they go out on a job. If they don't have a script or don't know all the details of the job, they feel as if they're going to be just fine if they're doing the show with him. If he can't do something, they're not going to get a dog to do it."

Real Name: Spooks
Breed: Mixed breed (part cocker spaniel, part poodle, part terrier)
Star Qualities: Stage fright. Spooks was afraid of everything, according to Frank Inn, but she overcame her fears to turn in dynamic performances.

Daisy looks on as *Blondie Takes a Vacation*. (*Archive Photos*)

Special Tricks: Among Spooks' large repertoire of tricks and behaviors was her ability to do a double take, a delayed reaction to a surprising event after initially failing to notice anything unusual.

Most Famous Role: Daisy in the *Blondie* film series. The first film, in 1938, spawned 27 sequels that kept theater audiences in stitches until 1950, including *Blondie Knows Best* (Columbia, 1946).

Plot of <u>Blondie Knows Best</u>

Dagwood Bumstead and Mr. Dithers switch identities in order to land an important construction contract. This leads to complications as Dagwood tries to avoid a process server and becomes a human guinea pig in a medical research experiment of truth serum.

Cast

Penny Singleton	Blondie
Arthur Lake	Dagwood
Larry Simms	Alexander
Marjorie Kent	Cookie

Jonathan Hale. . . . . J.C. Dithers
Shemp Howard. . . . . Process Server
Jerome Cowan . . . . Charles Peabody
Danny Mummert. . . . . Alvin Fuddle
Arthur Loft. . . . . Conroy
Ludwig Donath. . . . . Dr. Titus
Steven Geray . . . . Dr. Schmidt
Spooks. . . . . Daisy

Adventures Behind the Scenes

Cartoonist Chic Young created the comic strip "Blondie" for King Features Syndicate in 1930. It featured Dagwood Bumstead, the bumbling son of wealthy parents, and his girlfriend Blondie, a ditzy flapper. Through the thirties, Young chronicled their lives, including Dagwood and Blondie's marriage in 1933; Dagwood's being disowned by his father; and the couple starting a family with a son Baby Dumpling (later known as Alexander), a daughter Cookie, and the addition of an impish mutt named Daisy. In 1938, "Blondie" became a series of 28 low-budget episode films. Daisy provided additional laughs to audiences who chuckled at the antics of the Bumstead family.

Trainer Rennie Renfro found a dog in an animal shelter and asked Rudd Weatherwax to train her for the first Blondie film. "The dog was so nervous that Rennie called it Spooks. It was spooky of everything, but Rudd did such a good job training it," according to Frank Inn who trained some of Daisy's descendants during the run of the film series.

(The Museum of Modern Art/Film Stills Archive)

In addition to being able to do a double take, Daisy could also register surprise by raising her ears. For this trick, Daisy had the help of "invisible" wires to complete the illusion.

Frank Inn trained the double dog for Daisy, and this dog—called Daisy II—was an atmosphere or extra dog in the Elizabeth Taylor film *National Velvet*. Daisy II had to chase The Pie, causing the horse to jump over a fence. The scene also called for the dog to stop to scratch a flea, and Inn trained Daisy II to do this. Inn was so delighted with the scratching-the-flea effect that he and Daisy II enjoyed playing jokes on friends and passersby. "I had Daisy II follow about 25 feet behind me, no matter who I was walking with," Inn remembered. "When I stopped, I cued that dog to scratch a flea, and then I'd pay her for it." Daisy II's training at Inn's hands obviously made a realistic impression. Inn remembered that one time after a series of scratching-a-flea behaviors, a woman approached him, telling him that the dog was cute and that she could provide some powder to get rid of the fleas.

Several films in the *Blondie* series featured Daisy prominently. In 1940's *Blondie on a Budget*, Daisy doesn't realize the dangers of strong drink and becomes uproariously intoxicated. In 1942's *Blondie for Victory*, Daisy has a litter of puppies. In 1945's *Life with Blondie*, Daisy wins a Navy pinup contest, is dognapped by gangsters, and held for ransom.

Memorable Movie Moment

Because Dagwood has successfully eluded his efforts to serve him a summons, the process server bides his time by reading a newspaper while sitting on the low wall outside the Bumstead home, waiting for Dagwood to emerge. A paper boy bicycles down the street, arrives at the Bumstead home, and whistles at the house. Through the doggie door bounds Daisy who scurries down the front walk and takes a folded paper from the boy. Daisy turns to leave but is called back by the process server.

"Hey! Is your father in?"

Daisy shakes her head, and the process server does a double take. Daisy speeds toward the house, scoots through the doggie door, scampers to the kitchen, and places the paper on Dagwood's empty chair.

Notable Tidbits

In 1939, the Bumstead family, including Daisy, moved to radio for a series that lasted until 1950. The opening to each episode—"Uhh-uhh-uhh . . . don't touch that dial! Listen to . . . Blonnnndie!"—became a national catch phrase.

In 1957, seven years after the film and radio series had been retired, NBC turned the adventures of Blondie, Dagwood, and Daisy into a half-hour situation comedy series starring Arthur Lake (reprising his movie and radio role), Pamela Britton as Blondie, and a Daisy descendant playing the irrepressible pup. The series lasted only one season.

King Features Syndicate released the *Blondie* films to television in 1966 so that a new generation could enjoy the antics of the original Bumsteads and their precocious pooch.

In 1968, CBS tried another weekly television version of the Bumsteads. This time Will Hutchins (of *Sugarfoot* fame) starred as Dagwood, Patricia Harty as Blondie, and another Daisy descendant portrayed Daisy. Unfortunately, the series lasted a short five months.

Johnny Washbrook on Flicka. (*Movie Star News*)

FLICKA

Real Name: Wahama

Breed: Purebred Arabian

Star Qualities: Adaptable. Gentle-natured Wahama did any action required by trainer Les Hilton.

Special Tricks: The usual range of horse stunts: trotting, running, jumping, rearing, nickering, and nuzzling on cue.

Most Famous Role: Flicka in the television series *My Friend Flicka* (CBS, 1956–1958)

Story Line

In the rough and rugged turn-of-the-century West, Rob McLaughlin gives a once-wild horse, Flicka, to his son, Ken, to teach the boy responsibility. Episodes related Ken's adventures with Flicka—a Swedish name meaning "little girl"—and the family's struggles to earn a living from the land.

Cast

Gene Evans	Rob McLaughlin
Anita Louise	Nell McLaughlin
Johnny Washbrook	Ken McLaughlin
Frank Ferguson	Gus Broeberg
Pamela Beaird	Hildy Broeberg
	(1956)
Wahama	Flicka

Adventures Behind the Scenes

Based on the stories of novelist Mary O'Hara, Flicka's adventures graced both the silver and television screens. The film *My Friend Flicka*, starring Roddy McDowell, Preston Foster, and Rita Johnson, galloped onto the big screen in 1943, despite initial troubles.

The film's Twentieth Century-Fox production team decided to use untrained horses to hold down costs. The inexperienced equines were unruly and difficult to handle, causing many close calls with stunt people and multiple delays in filming. Finally, the studio decided that using experienced horse actors would be more cost effective, so legendary trainer Swede Lindell was hired to handle the animal action. Filming shut down for two weeks while Lindell worked his magic with his horses. When production resumed, the four horses that played Flicka hit their marks consistently, and filming proceeded without further delays or interruptions.

A well-known scene from the film involves Flicka charging toward and becoming entangled in a barbed-wire fence. Thousands of moviegoers were irate that such a beautiful animal was allowed to be mangled in such a cruel way and expressed their outraged complaints to the studio. In reality, the barbed-wire consisted of rubber bands and cork. *My Friend Flicka* led to a sequel, *Thunderhead, Son of Flicka*.

With the success of animal series on television, Twentieth Century-Fox once again corralled the Mary O'Hara stories and brought the adventures of Flicka to the television screen in the series, *My Friend Flicka*. Two nearly-identical horses were used for the series' 39 episodes. They were filmed in color but were originally broadcast in black-and-white in the late 1950s.

The lead horse for the series was Wahama, a six-year-old female purebred Arabian. Trainer Les Hilton, who worked both horses, felt that Wahama had a more gentle and adaptable nature. Hilton used Wahama for those scenes that called for tender emotion. Often actor Johnny Washbrook was Wahama's rider.

The second lead horse was Goldie, a fiesty five-year-old gelding who was the first foal of a Thoroughbred racehorse. Goldie was used in the action scenes. At the time, Hilton remarked that "he loves to buck off the baddies, but it makes him mad to have to learn anything new." Because Goldie was hard to handle, Washbrook was not permitted to ride the horse in scenes. Instead, Washbrook's double, a ten-year-old stunt girl, took over the reins for rough and tumble action.

Notable Tidbits

The television series *My Friend Flicka* enjoyed only moderate success in its initial television run. But because the series was shot in color, *My Friend Flicka* enjoyed re-run success for almost ten years.

FLIPPER

Real Name: Suzy/Cathy

Species: Bottlenose dolphin

Star Qualities: Intelligence. Suzy's trainer, Ricou Browning, observed the dolphin's problem-solving abilities firsthand. Once during training, he threw two different-sized balls into the water for Suzy to retrieve. She went after the big ball first, and when she tried to grab the small ball, the big one came out of her mouth. So she grabbed the small one first, but then she couldn't fit the big one in her mouth. In about two minutes, she figured out that she would be successful by going for the big ball first and then scooping the small one behind it.

Special Tricks: Carrying a boy on her back. Browning used the retrieving behavior as the basis for accomplishing this trick.

Most Famous Role: Flipper in the television series *Flipper* (NBC, 1964–1968)

Story Line

Flipper is the pet of 15-year-old Sandy and 10-year-old Bud, sons of Porter Ricks, chief ranger of Coral Key Park. Ranger Ricks is responsible for protecting both game fish and water enthusiasts in the Florida park. Episodes related the adventures of the boys and their aquatic pet who rescued them from many perilous situations.

Cast

Brian Kelly . . . . Porter Ricks
Luke Halpin . . . . Sandy Ricks

Tommy Norden .... Bud Ricks
Andy Devine .... Hap Gorman
(1964–1965)
Ulla Stromstedt... Ulla Norstrand
(1965–1966)
Suzy/Cathy .... Flipper

Adventures Behind the Scenes

Underwater stuntman Ricou Browning was inspired to create the character Flipper while watching another animal actor performing. "As I was watching *Lassie* on television with my kids, I thought, wouldn't it be great to do an animal show similar to *Lassie* with a kid and a dolphin?" Browning said. That idea sparked the thought of writing a book about a boy and a dolphin, which took about four months for Browning and a collaborator friend. They titled the work *Flipper*, then Browning headed for New York City to try to interest a publisher in the project. He was turned down wherever he went.

Undaunted, Browning thought that if he could get a movie producer to express interest in making his book into a film, a book publisher would be more willing to publish the novel. Having done stunt work on the television series *Sea Hunt*, Browning telephoned the program's producer Ivan Tors, told him about his book project, and asked if he would agree to read the manuscript. Tors agreed. Several weeks later, Browning received a telephone call from the producer. "Let's make a movie of *Flipper*, that story of yours," Tors told him. Tors authorized Browning to find a dolphin for the role of Flipper.

Browning visited aquariums throughout Florida and across the United States in search of a dolphin. He soon realized that dolphin shows featured land-based trainers working with dolphins in the water. In his Flipper story, a boy rode a dolphin, but Browning did not know of any actual instance of a person riding a dolphin. When Browning got into the water with the dolphins he encountered at aquariums, they swam away in fear.

Through his contacts at the aquariums, Browning heard about Milton Santini, a dolphin supplier located in the Florida Keys. Santini owned a pet dolphin named Mitzi who willingly shared the space of her pool with human beings. Browning and Tors visited Santini. As soon as Browning entered the pool, the dolphin swam over to him and even allowed him to hold her in his arms. "We decided immediately that this was the animal we were going to use for Flipper and negotiated a deal with Santini," Browning said.

Browning moved to the Florida Keys with his son, Ricky, so that Mitzi could begin training for the required stunts. Warned by trainers that some stunts would take six months to a year for Mitzi to learn, Browning was surprised at how quickly the dolphin accomplished her behaviors, especially retrieving. She retrieved sticks, balls, and just about any object that she was able to carry. She could tow a boat with a rope, hit the water with her tail, and shake hands with her flipper. But after weeks of training with the help of nine-year-old Ricky, Mitzi was still not able to perform one of the major stunts of the film—carrying a boy on her back.

Then Browning had a brilliant idea. What if he used the retrieving behavior to achieve the desired effect? Browning decided to try with Ricky's assistance. He picked up his son,

Luke Halpin (Sandy Ricks) and Flipper. (*Archive Photos*)

ordered Mitzi to fetch, then threw the boy into the water about four feet from the dock. Mitzi swam to him, grabbed an unbuckled strap on the back of the child's cut off blue jeans, and pulled Ricky until she lost her grip on the strap. Ricky placed his arm over the top of Mitzi's fin, and she pushed him to the dock. Browning rewarded her then threw Ricky in again. "This time she swam to him and immediately put her fin right into his arm where his elbow bends. I yelled to him, 'Grab her fins!' He did, and she immediately pulled him back to me. As far as I know that's the first time a trained dolphin had ever done that," Browning said.

Once Mitzi had learned all of the required tricks and behaviors, shooting on the movie *Flipper* began. Mitzi was afraid of the buzz made by the underwater camera and the whirring made by the running outboard motors. To get her used to the buzz, a motor that made a similar sound was placed in the water and allowed to run. To get her used to the whirring, a protective cage was placed around the boat's propeller, and the engine was left on. She became acclimated to the sounds within a day.

The land shots and underwater sequences for the feature film *Flipper* (1963) and the sequel *Flipper's New Adventures* (1964) were filmed in the Bahamas. Mitzi starred in each film, but when the decision was made to move forward with a television series, the production team acquired a new dolphin, Suzy, from the Miami Seaquarium. Land shots for the television series were filmed in Florida while the underwater sequences with Suzy were shot in the Bahamas. Browning trained Suzy as lead dolphin for the television series. Four other trainers trained four other dolphins as stand-ins for Suzy, including a dolphin named Cathy. "These animals were so highly intelligent that they soon could do 35 to 40 behaviors, and that was all that we needed for just about any script circumstance," Browning said.

Luke Halpin, who starred in both Flipper films and in the Flipper television series, had special moments with Suzy. Before he dove with Suzy, Halpin took a gulp of air from the surface then plunged beneath the water, holding onto the dolphin as she headed down toward the bottom. Halpin noticed that whenever he needed more air, the dolphin returned to the surface. Because Suzy repeated this behavior regularly, it occurred to Halpin that with her keen hearing and sonar ability she was probably monitoring his heart and respiration rates and knew when he needed air.

At the end of a day of filming, Suzy sometimes swam into Halpin's arms and slept for a few minutes. At other times, she just leaned against him, enjoying his company. But sometimes a jovial side came out which frightened Halpin half to death. "She would come swimming at me from out of the blue—out of nowhere—going a hundred miles an hour, swimming right for my face mask. Then she'd come to a dead stop right in front of me. She was just playing; just scaring me," Halpin said.

Suzy also joked with producer Ivan Tors. She had learned a new stunt—squirting water—and probably was anxious to show off her stuff to the big boss. On a visit to the location, when Tors walked down to the dock and greeted Suzy, she squirted water and soaked his shoes. Those who caught the stunt roared, and Tors got a kick out of it as well.

As intelligent as dolphins are, Browning did not realize that deviations from an animal's stunt would have serious consequences. Suzy had been trained to carry Tommy Norden and Luke Halpin from one place to another and then to the trainer for a fish reward. But one scene in the script called for Norden to ride Suzy down through the water, to have him see something, let go of the dolphin, and swim away. When Norden swam away, Suzy followed and nudged him. She thought that the only way she would get rewarded was to carry him to the trainer. When he kept swimming, Suzy hit him harder, and then she hit him again. Norden grabbed hold of Suzy and allowed the dolphin to carry him to the trainer. The trainer rewarded her with a piece of fish. According to Browning, this taught Suzy that if she hit the actor, he would hold on to her. Shortly thereafter, in another scene, Suzy hit Luke Halpin. Frightened that the dolphin would hurt Halpin, the trainer threw a fish to distract Suzy. According to Browning, this taught Suzy that hitting someone would result in a reward. "What we were doing was screwing up the dolphin's training, and we didn't know how to correct what we'd done," Browning said. Suzy's behavior with the young actors became so rough that Browning decided to retire her to the Seaquarium before she seriously injured them. Her stand-in, Cathy, then became the star of Flipper.

A favorite scene in the original movie was repeated with some variation in the television series—Flipper battling and killing a shark to save one of the boys. This scene was orchestrated with a real dolphin, a real shark, a six-foot-long fiberglass dolphin, and a nine-foot-long fiberglass shark. The crew filmed the real shark confronting the fiberglass dolphin, then the real dolphin confronting the fiberglass shark, then the real shark and the real dolphin encountering each other. "When we edited all of that film together, we had the damnedest fight you ever saw, and we made it appear as if the dolphin killed the shark," Browning said.

Notable Tidbits

Flipper wasn't alone in breaking into show business with underwater talents. The break for Ricou Browning, Flipper's creator and trainer, was the role of the creature in *The Creature From the Black Lagoon* (1954). The film's production team thought his style of swimming was unusual and hired him for the role after viewing test film they had shot of him while scouting Wakulla Springs, Florida, as a potential underwater location for their movie. Ricou performed stunt and underwater work in *Twenty Thousand Leagues under the Sea* (1954), *Don't Give Up the Ship* (1959), and in the 1960s television series *Sea Hunt*.

Flipper was a three-time PATSY Award winner in 1965, 1966, and 1967.

Flipper made a cameo appearance in Elvis Presley's 1967 movie *Clambake*, which was set in Florida. Flipper surfaced, chattered briefly, then dove back into the water.

Flipper returned to television in 1995 in the syndicated series *Flipper*, starring Jessica Marie Alba, Colleen Flynn, Payton Haas, and Brian Wimmer. The role of Flipper was played by a dolphin named Slim and three backups. Flipper also hit the silver screen in *Flipper*, the 1996 Universal Pictures film starring Elijah Wood and Paul Hogan. In this film, the role of Flipper was played by three live dolphins—Jake, Fat Man, and McGuyver—and a life-size animatronic dolphin.

FRANCIS
THE TALKING MULE

Real Name: Molly

Species: Mule (offspring of a male donkey and female horse)

Star Qualities: Good natured but with a stubborn streak. Molly good naturedly performed almost all of the stunts required for the *Francis* film series, but absolutely refused to sit. For that behavior, trainer Les Hilton used a mule double. Molly had three other stand-ins to assist with long shots.

Special Tricks: Molly could climb stairs, loosen a rope with her teeth, and wink on cue.

Most Famous Role: Francis in a series of six films, including *Francis Joins the WACs* (Universal, 1954)

Plot of <u>Francis Joins the WACs</u>

As a result of an Army snafu, bumbling but sincere Peter Stirling and smart yet sassy Army mule Francis are assigned to a Women's Army Corp base. Together, the pair whip into shape an unruly platoon in time to compete in a camouflage demonstration organized by a wily general who wants to prove that women soldiers are inferior to men soldiers. Thanks to Francis' clever field strategy and a supply of smoke grenades, the WACs win the competition and teach the general a valuable lesson.

Cast

Donald O'Connor	Peter Stirling
Julia Adams	Captain Jane Parker
Mamie Van Doren	Corporal Bunky Hilstrom
Lynn Bari	Major Louise Simpson
Zasu Pitts	Lt. Valerie Humpert
Mara Corday	Kate
Allison Hayes	Lt. Dickson
Joan Shawlee	Sgt. Kip
Chill Wills	General Ben Kaye and the Voice of Francis
Molly	Francis

Adventures Behind the Scenes

Francis the Talking Mule was the featured character in the David Stern novel, *Francis*, which was adapted into a screenplay in 1949. Director Arthur Lubin (who went on to create the *Mr. Ed* television series) acquired the rights and sold the project to Universal Pictures, which was looking for a vehicle for singer/dancer Donald O'Connor. The studio launched a nationwide search for a mule to star as Francis. Molly, who was untrained yet photogenic and easy to handle, won the role. Universal Pictures paid $350 for Molly.

Molly was trained by Les Hilton, who later worked on the *Mr. Ed* television series. Initially, Hilton gave Molly chewing gum and then chewing tobacco to make the mule move her mouth to simulate talking. When those efforts failed, Hilton fashioned the mule's bridle with strong thread which fed into her mouth. When Hilton pulled the thread, Molly tried to dislodge it by moving her lips. At other times, Hilton pressed the muscles on the side of Molly's face, causing her to move her lips. Thus, Francis appeared to talk.

Director Arthur Lubin wanted Francis to have a Western twang in his voice. Chill Wills, a character actor in numerous Westerns of the Thirties and Forties, was selected to provide the voice. Wills had an affinity for mules since he had been a mule skinner (or a driver of mules) in the Oklahoma oil fields in his pre-Hollywood days. He felt a special connec-

tion to Francis such that he sometimes ignored the script and ad-libbed the mule's dialogue. Wills's only on-screen appearance in a Francis movie was in *Francis Joins the WACs*, in which he appeared as General Ben Kaye. In fact, his first line in the film poked fun at his role in the series: "Major, you might think that I'm a stubborn mule. Just because a few of your women have developed into adequate camouflage specialists, it doesn't mean that you can flood the service with them." Actor Paul Frees replaced Wills as the voice of Francis in *Francis in the Haunted House* (1956).

Between the first Francis film and the second, Molly put on the old feedbag big time. In fact, she gained so much weight that the studio ordered her to lose at least 200 excess

Francis Goes to the Races

pounds. Her diet was adjusted from oat hay to alfalfa. Tied to a station wagon, Molly jogged up and down the hills of Hollywood and lost 100 pounds; she sweated off the next hundred in a custom-made steam cabinet.

Francis was the star of seven films: *Francis* (1950), *Francis Goes to the Races* (1951), *Francis Goes to West Point* (1952), *Francis Covers the Big Town* (1953), *Francis Joins the WACs* (1954), *Francis in the Navy* (1955), *Francis in the Haunted House* (1956). For the last film, Donald O'Connor bid adieu to Francis and was replaced by Mickey Rooney. Over the course of the film series, Francis made millions of dollars for Universal Pictures.

Memorable Movie Moment

General Kaye doesn't believe that Francis has spoken to both Major Simpson and Captain Parker so, accompanied by those officers, the General visits Francis in the barn.

"So you're the talking mule, huh?" the General says. "All right. Talk it up."

Francis is silent. The General waits.

"This is all utter nonsense," the General turns to leave.

"What do you mean 'utter nonsense'?" Francis asks and blows his lips in a mule version of the raspberries.

At first, the General is incredulous, but then he gives Francis permission to sound off.

"Well, to start with you're a narrow-minded fuddy-duddy," Francis tells him. "You probably think the top brass is the machinery that runs this man's army. Horse feathers! Now you take these WACs. Everyone knows that women are here to stay. Not you. You've got the idea they're in the service just to keep your memos circulating."

Before Francis can continue sounding off, Peter Stirling (who has been hiding in the stall) tumbles out. The General accuses him of being a ventriloquist and orders him to the psychiatric ward.

Notable Tidbits

Francis was the first animal to win a PATSY Award when the awards were introduced in 1951. Francis captured the award five more times in 1952, 1954, 1955, 1956, and 1957.

Real Name: Lala

Species: Cockatoo

Star Qualities: Intelligence. Although cockatoos are usually intelligent, Lala was exceptionally smart. He could learn a new behavior in as little as five minutes.

Special Tricks: Lala's specialty was lying on his back and "drinking" from a bottle of booze. Trainer Ray Berwick coached this behavior by filling a bottle with sunflower seeds. For Lala to get to them, he had to roll over, hold the bottle with his legs, then tip the bottle upside down.

Most Famous Role: Fred in the television series *Baretta* (ABC, 1975–1978)

Story Line

Pugnacious police detective Tony Baretta fights crime in the big city. Episodes related Baretta's exploits as a street-wise cop and his friendship with his pet cockatoo, Fred.

Cast

Robert Blake . . . . Tony Baretta
Tom Ewell . . . . Billy Truman

Dana Elcar . . . . Inspector Shiller
(1975)
Edward Grover. . . . . Lt. Hal Brubaker
Michael D. Roberts. . . . . Rooster
Chino Williams. . . . . Fats
Lala. . . . . Fred

Adventures Behind the Scenes

Bird expert Ray Berwick (*The Birds*, *Birdman of Alcatraz*) found Lala, a milk-white cockatoo, in Hong Kong and brought the young bird to the United States. At the time, Lala spoke only Chinese. Berwick taught the bird English, trained Lala to perform a repertoire of tricks, and sought a Hollywood career for the intelligent and beautiful bird.

When the production team for *Baretta* was planning the show, Baretta was characterized as a loner who confided his innermost thoughts to a picture of a mynah bird. Wouldn't it be better, someone suggested, to use a real mynah bird instead of a picture? A casting call was announced for mynahs. Berwick brought a mynah to the audition and also brought along Lala. When star Robert Blake saw Lala kiss, wave, and imitate a barking dog, he was sold. "We go with the talent," Blake said, and he hired Lala for the role of Fred.

During the series, Lala had a stand-in named Weird Harold who performed flying stunts. Lala performed the other tricks such as doing a cartwheel,

(*Archive Photos/fotos international*)

talking back on cue, or perching on Robert Blake's head or arm. According to Berwick, Lala didn't trust Blake, and this was evident in one scene in which Fred was to hang upside down on Baretta's fingers. "We rehearsed it with me carrying him upside down, but he refused to let go and give himself up to Blake, because he thought he might drop him," Berwick said. Blake grabbed the bird from Berwick, and Fred yelled "Help! Help! Don't hurt Fred!" three times. Berwick was astounded because he had not taught the bird to say those words.

Lala resented being handled by people who were unskilled in working with birds. Once, Robert Blake began waving his hands around, pretending to give commands to Lala. The bird refused to put up with such nonsense and went on the offensive by chasing Blake around the room and pecking him.

Notable Tidbits

Lala's popularity on *Baretta*—the bird received more fan mail than Robert Blake—started a trend in owning pet birds during the late 1970s. *Newsweek* estimated that 40 million people owned at least one bird. Although canaries and parakeets were the most popular, exotic birds such as macaws, Amazon and African gray parrots, toucans, and cockatoos became especially sought after as people tried for a relationship similar to that of Baretta and Fred.

As Fred, Lala was awarded two consecutive Grand PATSY Awards in 1976 and 1977. In 1977, *Photoplay* named Lala "Favorite Live Animal Star" and bestowed their Gold Medal award.

Real Name: Highland Dale (officially); nicknamed Beauty

Breed: American saddle horse

Star Qualities: Quick learner. According to owner and trainer Ralph McCutcheon, Beauty was astounding in his aptitude for learning. McCutcheon needed only to rehearse a new trick twice and Beauty was ready for a take.

Special Tricks: Among Beauty's repertoire of tricks were limping, kneeling, lying down, playing dead, grinning, fetching, untying knots and opening doors with his mouth, poking his head through open windows, and allowing himself to be chased.

Most Famous Role: Fury in the television series *Fury* (NBC, 1955–1960)

Story Line

As the young owner of the Broken Wheel Ranch, widower Jim Newton specializes in capturing and taming wild range horses. He befriends a tough city kid, Joey, and invites the

The cast of *Fury*: William Fawcett, Bobby Diamond, Fury (Beauty), and Peter Graves.

boy to make his home at the ranch, overseen by Pete, a weathered ranch hand. Although Joey's adjustment to ranch life is difficult at first, he finds a kindred spirit in Jim's newest captive, a black stallion called Fury. Each episode of this contemporary Western related "the story of a horse and the boy who loved him."

Cast

Peter Graves	Jim Newton
Bobby Diamond	Joey
William Fawcett	Pete
Jimmy Baird	Pee Wee Jenkins
Roger Mobley	Packey Lambert
Beauty	Fury

Adventures Behind the Scenes

Highland Dale was a Hollywood horse veteran by the time the *Fury* series debuted on Saturday morning network television in 1955. Born and raised on a Missouri farm, the horse made his debut in 1946 in *Black Beauty*, starring Richard Denning and Mona Freeman. The film was an adaptation of English writer Anna Sewell's novel of a little girl and her love for her horse. The cast, crew, and Highland Dale's trainer referred to the horse as Beauty throughout the making of the film, and the nickname stuck.

Beauty also served as Clark Gable's horse in *Lone Star* (1952), Joan Crawford's mount in *Johnny Guitar* (1954), and Elizabeth Taylor's ride in *Giant* (1956). In 1954, Beauty had the lead in *Gypsy Colt* with Donna Corcoran and Ward Bond, where he played a faithful horse who finds his way back to his mistress after being sold by her parents to a racing stable. For that performance, Beauty won a PATSY.

Beauty had an uncanny ability to learn a trick or routine quickly and then be ready for the camera. For example, when a script called for Beauty to chase a movie bad guy then kick a package out of his hand without harming the actor, Beauty breezed through two rehearsals and performed the routine perfectly when the cameras rolled.

When the young girl who doubled for Bobby Diamond began to blossom into a young lady, trainer Ralph McCutcheon recommended a buddy of his as a replacement. Slightly built Whitey Hughes was an expert at riding "falling" horses, the animals that took the tumbles during climactic scenes. According to Hughes, "I had 'em on me about as much as I've been on them." Hughes rode the extra horses that were used in the series. "We had a chase horse that I did all the chases on, the stuff that was really rugged because naturally they wouldn't use Fury and take a chance on getting him hurt," Hughes said. McCutcheon and Hughes had similar voices, and Hughes was able to imitate McCutcheon's voice so well that Beauty was fooled into thinking that the voice was that of his trainer. This never ceased to crack up cast and crew.

The closing scene from many episodes of *Fury* brought Jim, Pete, and Joey together to comment on the goodness of life, while Joey petted Fury. "That was our tag line," Peter Graves (who played Jim Newton) said. "*Fury* was a series of little Aesop's Fables, timeless stories on the benefits of the outdoor life. Every show taught something; they were constructed that way, to always teach a little lesson."

Beauty earned $1,500 per episode for *Fury*. As part of Beauty's contract, trainer McCutcheon asked for and received five percent of the series' profits which, after its long run on NBC, went into syndication as *Brave Stallion*. When Beauty retired, he ranked second only to Lassie in net income earned by an animal actor.

Notable Tidbits

Beauty won PATSY Awards in 1960 and 1961 for his role as Fury.

Gentle Ben

Real Name: Bruno
Species: Black bear
Star Qualities: Craved affection. "If he doesn't get affection, he comes to a slitherin' halt," according to Bruno's trainer, Monty Cox. When Bruno slipped out of his usually good mood, Cox brought him to his Miami apartment where they shared a meal, showered, and turned in for the night. Cox's only complaint was that Bruno never stayed on his side of the bed.
Special Tricks: Although bears tend to be unusually shy, Bruno was extremely friendly. One of his best pals was the dolphin who played Flipper, and the two enjoyed swimming together.
Most Famous Role: Ben in the television series *Gentle Ben* (CBS, 1967–1969)

Story Line

The son of a wildlife officer, a small boy befriends a bear who then becomes a member of the family. Episodes related their adventures in the Florida Everglades.

Cast

Dennis Weaver	Tom Wedloe
Clint Howard	Mark Wedloe
Beth Brickell	Ellen Wedloe
Rance Howard	Henry Boomhauer
Angelo Rutherford	Willie (1968–1969)
Bruno	Ben

Adventures Behind the Scenes

Orphaned as cubs, Bruno and his brother Smokey were half grown when they found a home at Africa, USA, an affection-training animal compound near Los Angeles founded by animal trainer Ralph Helfer and producer Ivan Tors (*Flipper*, *Daktari*). Tors cast Bruno in the feature films *Zebra in the Kitchen* (1965) and in *Gentle Giant* (1967). In reviewing *Gentle Giant*, Howard Thompson of the *New York Times* wrote that "Ben, the bear is a pretty wonderful old critter." The success of the film and the appeal of Bruno as Ben lead to the television series, *Gentle Ben.*

Bruno's claim to fame was his gentleness. According to Ricou Browning who directed some of the episodes, "It was difficult filming him because he wasn't well trained. We had other bears, some trained better than him, that we used as doubles and backups, and also for stunts and tricks. Gentle Ben's main capacity in the show was

Clint Howard with Gentle Ben (Bruno). (*Archive Photos*)

to work with the boy and to be friendly and nice."

Bruno's human co-star, young Clint Howard, hit it right off with the big bruin. At the time Howard said: "He's as gentle as my cat Mitts. It doesn't matter how big he is; I'm not afraid of him, and he's not afraid of me." Howard was even forgiving when Bruno accidentally stepped on his foot. Tears welled in the boy's eyes, but he didn't cry, and he continued the scene.

Bruno tipped the scales at nearly 650 pounds. For his regular daily fare, he consumed five loaves of bread, a few bunches of carrots, almost three pounds of a prepared "bear chow," a half dozen apples and oranges, a fatty acid (Bucatone) to maintain his coat, Vionate powder, and a regimen of vitamins and minerals. He was addicted to sweets, especially the soft drinks, candy, and doughnuts he mooched from anyone who offered to feed him. He also had a well-known passion for lemon drops. During a photo shoot, producer Ivan Tors needed Bruno to "kiss" him for a cute shot. Tors placed a lemon drop behind his ear, Bruno licked his face to get to the candy, and the action looked like a kiss. During a press conference, Bruno stayed quiet and close to Tors as he addressed the media. Bruno knew that the producer had a pocketful of lemon drops, and the bear wanted to guard the cache that he hoped would sooner or later be his.

Even when Bruno wasn't supposed to eat, he ate. One scene required Ben to be off his food. To ensure this, chief trainer Monty Cox stuffed Bruno beforehand with twelve loaves of bread, ten apples, ten oranges, ten carrots, and a gallon of milk. Thinking that would do the trick, the director called for the shot. "Everytime we started to shoot, he'd eat again," Cox said. "So we put cold cream on the food and Chanel No. 5. Just to discourage him. But he still ate it. He smelled good for quite a while."

Eating the equivalent of small grocery stores didn't seem to make Bruno the least bit lethargic, but working in the humid Florida heat did. At those times, he was hard to motivate through a scene, so Cox brought on Bruno's double, Buck. Bruno's other two stand-ins were used when the director needed Ben to run or to fight. Despite his outgoing nature and affinity for humans, Bruno didn't like to run—although he loved to wrestle—and never learned any movie or television stunts.

Notable Tidbits

Bruno won a PATSY Award in 1968 for his work in *Gentle Giant*.

J. FRED MUGGS

Real Name: Mr. Muggs (originally)

Species: Chimpanzee

Star Qualities: Intelligence. According to co-owner and trainer Buddy Mennella, J. Fred Muggs was raised to understand words and was especially intelligent. "You could put thirty pieces of different fruits and vegetables in front of him and ask him for each one of them individually by name and he'd give them to you," Mennella said.

Special Tricks: J. Fred Muggs was an expert at celebrity impersonations. Among his repertoire were Jack Benny, Popeye the Sailor, General George Patton, Richard Nixon, Ed Sullivan, Jackie Gleason, Jimmy Durante, and Groucho Marx.

Most Famous Role: J. Fred Muggs on the *Today Show* from 1953 to 1957 (NBC, debuted in 1952)

Description

The *Today Show* is a live, daily, two-hour news and information television program. When J. Fred Muggs was featured on the show, cast members included Dave Garroway, Jack Lescoulie, and Frank Blair.

Adventures Behind the Scenes

Buddy Mennella and Roy Waldron were pages at NBC and later became partners in a New Jersey pet store. In 1952, on an excursion to New York City to acquire stock for the store, Mennella purchased a 13-week-old chimpanzee for $600 from Henry Trefflich, a well-known animal supplier. "I loved apes, and I couldn't wait to own one," Mennella said. But he didn't intend to resell the chimpanzee in the pet shop. Mennella wanted the ape as a pet. "He soon became one of the family," Mennella said.

Every day the chimp accompanied Mennella and Waldron to their

The adorable J. Fred Muggs at eleven months old. (*Archive Photos*)

pet store. The ape was so appealing that customers brought in hand-me-down clothing for him to wear. Then the partners decided to sponsor a name-the-chimp contest open to children between the ages of six and fourteen. The winning entry was "Mr. Muggs," a name submitted by a boy.

Mr. Muggs' first television appearance was on *The Children's Hour*, a locally broadcast Saturday morning program. Mr. Muggs appeared in a sixteen-minute film clip, showing him interacting and playing with a group of children.

While visiting their old stomping grounds at NBC, Mennella, Waldron, and Mr. Muggs were spotted by a staff member from the *Today Show*. The trio was ushered into the office of one of the producers, and the partners were asked to allow Mr. Muggs to make an appearance on the *Today Show*. They agreed to have the chimpanzee appear for $50. Before Mennella and Waldron left NBC that day, they visited another old friend, Perry Como, who had his own network television show. Como invited the partners and Mr. Muggs on stage for the audience warm up, then the star borrowed the chimpanzee for one of the songs he sang in the show. Como sang "Jambalaya" while cuddling Mr. Muggs in his arms. This was the chimpanzee's first network television appearance.

Because of a defective alarm clock and icy roads, Mr. Muggs missed his February 1953 *Today Show* appearance. By the time he and his owners arrived at the studio, the show had already aired, and they were told that they had blown their chance. "Feeling rather dejected, we went down to the drugstore to get a cup of coffee," Mennella remembered. "Muggs was sitting there with us. Within ten minutes the *Today* people were searching that whole building looking for us. They grabbed us bodily—poor Muggs never got to finish his doughnut— and rushed us upstairs to an office. Before that day was over, we had a five-year contract." And Mr. Muggs had a different name. Mennella and Waldron added the first name "J. Fred" because it gave him "an air of distinction."

For J. Fred Muggs, his *Today* began at 4 a.m. He arrived at the studio by 6 a.m., was on camera for the entire two-hour program, then spent additional hours posing for publicity shots. While the chimpanzee was on camera, Mennella was off camera nearby to oversee J. Fred's handling. Sometimes J. Fred Muggs sat peacefully with host Dave Garroway, and at other times the chimp ran wild on the set in a bit called "The Chase." According to Mennella, J. Fred earned $200 a week.

J. Fred Muggs acquired a wardrobe of 450 outfits for his television work and personal appearances. He had worn clothes his entire life and enjoyed dressing up, but he disliked long sleeves. He tolerated a long-sleeved garment only for so long then he stripped it off. J. Fred Muggs was toilet trained, but to be on the safe side, he wore a diaper and rubber pants with each outfit.

Muggs was instrumental in helping the fledgling *Today Show* gain an audience and get into the black financially. According to a network number cruncher: "The net result was we returned from a loss of $1.7 million a year to a profit of $2 million on a gross of $10 million on the first full fiscal year—after six months of getting organized."

J. Fred Muggs created many funny and memorable moments for the *Today Show*. Once when actress Anita Ekberg was a guest, she invited J. Fred to sit on her lap. The young ape looked up at her, noticed her clip-on earrings, and touched one of them. The earring, not securely in place, fell off her ear and into her bosom. J. Fred reached in, retrieved the earring, and returned it to Ekberg. "She just adored him," Mennella said.

Notable Tidbits

J. Fred Muggs completed a round-the-world tour with his owners, and he was allowed to ride in the passenger compartment. "The airlines made the exception to the rule with him because he was so good on a plane," Mennella said.

In 1955, J. Fred Muggs had a role in the Bob Hope film *The Seven Little Foys*. After his stint on the *Today Show*, J. Fred Muggs starred in his own local television show called *The J. Fred Muggs Show*. Later he worked for nearly four years at Busch Gardens in Tampa, Florida. Included in his act was a fencing demonstration, a manual of arms routine, and a number in which J. Fred played a set of octave bells to the tune "The Bells of Saint Mary's."

In addition to being an entertainer, J. Fred Muggs was an accomplished finger-painter. He completed more than 10,000 paintings, one of which became a cover for *Mad* magazine.

J. Fred Muggs celebrates his second birthday in 1954. (*Archive Photos*)

JERRY LEE

Real Name: Rando
Breed: German shepherd
Star Qualities: "A strong heart and willingness to please," according to trainer Karl Lewis Miller.
Special Tricks: Growling and snarling on command, jumping through an open car window, leaping from the top of one building to the top of the building next door.
Most Famous Role: Jerry Lee in *K-9* (Universal, 1989)

Plot

A loose-cannon narcotics investigator and a chili-eating, drug-sniffing German shepherd team up to bring down a drug kingpin.

Cast

James Belushi. . . . . Dooley
Mel Harris . . . . Tracy
Kevin Tighe . . . . Lyman
Ed O'Neill . . . . Brannigan
James Handy . . . . Byers
Daniel Davis . . . . Halstaad
Rando . . . . Jerry Lee

Adventures Behind the Scenes

According to Karl Lewis Miller, the production team at Universal looked at practically every trained German shepherd in the industry but couldn't find a dog with the right personality for the role of Jerry Lee. Time was growing short. A dog had to be found. Miller knew that Mark Mooring, the film's technical advisor and a canine officer with the Los Angeles Police Department, had European contacts for procuring German shepherds for police work. Miller suggested that Universal send Mooring to Germany to acquire three look-alike dogs and transport them back to the States. Miller agreed to train all the dogs equally, hoping that one would have the personality the studio wanted. Miller insisted that the dogs be of the same caliber as good police dogs and be old enough to have had some protection training. Subsequently, three likely prospects arrived in Los Angeles.

Miller had a unique problem. Although the dogs were fully trained, they understood commands only in German. For example, the dogs might react to the German command

(*Archive Photos/fotos international*)

"*platz*" by lying down (as long as the pronunciation was exactly the same as they had learned from their original trainer), but they had no clue what the English command "down" meant. "I had to teach them English," Miller explained. Fortunately, hand signals and body gestures used in dog training are universal. "We just started using English but emphasizing the body motions and the hand signals," Miller said. "Therefore, they picked up a whole new sound system."

Miller had 12 weeks to train the 18-month-old dogs for the film. "This was quite a challenge for everything the dog had to do," Miller said. In the script, one dog was called upon to perform almost all the animal action that Lassie, Rin Tin Tin, and Benji had done during their entire careers. In the eleventh week of training, a writers' strike erupted, and the film was delayed. Because the studio did not know how long the strike would last, Universal decided to keep the dogs in training. "We ended up with about twenty-six weeks of prep," Miller said. That level of preparation enabled the film to be completed one day ahead of schedule—unheard of in a film with animal action.

According to Miller, director Rod Daniel went out of his way to accommodate Rando. Daniel consulted Miller each morning before the day's shooting began, so that the director could understand how Rando would perform a stunt, where Miller had to be positioned for the trick, and the manner in which the trainer would cue the animal. "Instead of setting up shots and forcing me to make the dog do it his way, he took the time to set up the shots for the dog. Then he'd call in the crew and tell them that this was the way they had to do it," Miller said.

Actor James Belushi interacted with Rando between scenes to make certain that their on-camera work looked realistic. "Jim communicated with that dog, and the dog responded to him," Miller said. The kitchen scene in which Dooley tries to intimidate Jerry Lee, and the two end up wrestling on the floor was one of the more difficult to do, according to Miller. "We couldn't force the wrestling stuff on the dog because if Jim got too heavy and hard in his acting, it would scare the dog, and the dog would run away and not want to come back," Miller said. "Jim took his time, sitting with the dog, rolling him, rocking him, flipping him, and just building up a little play thing. As the dog gained confidence that he wouldn't be hurt or thrown around too much, the dog tolerated more and more. The two of them ad libbed a phony wrestling match."   Miller estimates that about four hours of footage was shot for a scene that appears for 45 seconds on the screen.

To prepare for the scene in which Jerry Lee rides through the car wash in an open Mustang convertible, the harsh detergent was replaced with baby shampoo, and the brushes and water-removing mechanisms were disabled. To make doubly sure that the scene would be safe, Miller and the on-site representative from the American Humane Association rode through the carwash themselves. "It was safe enough for us, so it was safe enough for the dog," Miller said. For Rando's ride, he was strapped in with a hidden safety harness so he couldn't jump out.

The roof top scene originally called for no cuts. The top door was to burst open, and Jerry Lee was to run through the door with Dooley following; Jerry Lee was to run toward the edge of the building, leap across and land on the roof top of the other building. But Miller objected because he didn't think it was safe for the dog. Miller, the director, and the cameraman had a quick consultation and arrived at a solution that pleased everyone. Two dogs were used for the shot in one take. One dog ran up the stairs, through the door, and along the roof top. The second dog, waiting on the roof top just out of camera range, was released to do the jump. According to Miller, a dangerous stunt was transformed into a predictable trick.

Memorable Movie Moment

After Jerry Lee saves him from the roughnecks in the bar, Dooley decides to continue their partnership but with one proviso.

"You stink. This car stinks, you know that? If we're going to be spending some time together, I got to deodorize [you]," Dooley tells Jerry Lee as they cruise to a supermarket in Dooley's 1965 Mustang convertible.

Dooley buys a can of dry shampoo and a doggy deodorant guaranteed to make Jerry Lee smell like cedar chips. Jerry Lee objects to being sprayed with the aerosol deodorant, grabs the can from Dooley, and demolishes it with his teeth.

"All right. If that's what you want, that's the way you're going to have it," Dooley says.

Dooley pulls the Mustang into an automatic car wash. He sends the car through with the top down and with Jerry Lee in the front passenger seat. Dooley is delighted as Jerry Lee gets soaped and rinsed by the machinery and then towel dried at the end by the attendants.

"You smell good, but I'd like cedar chips," Dooley tells Jerry Lee as the car exits the washing bay. "Well, that concludes today's lesson."

Not quite. Jerry Lee barks at Dooley, yanks out the radio communication system from beneath the dashboard, then drops it with a thud on the floor of the Mustang.

Notable Tidbits

Rando retired from movie making after *K-9* and became a house pet. According to Miller, Rando became fat and sassy and enjoyed running on the beaches of Malibu.

Real Name: Judy
Species: Chimpanzee
Star Qualities: One-take wonder. Adept at acting, Judy usually performed her tricks proficiently in one take. She became annoyed with human actors who took too long to rehearse, and when they were ready for the shot, she refused to work. She could be persuaded to get back to business with a cup of ice cream.
Special Tricks: Judy knew how to pick locks and often used this skill to set free animals confined in cages.
Most Famous Role: Judy in the television series *Daktari* (CBS, 1966–1969)

Story Line

An American veterinarian and his daughter run an animal study center in Africa. Episodes related their adventures with natives, poachers, and animals, including their pets, a lion and a chimpanzee.

Cast

Marshall Thompson	Dr. Marsh Tracy
Cheryl Miller	Paula Tracy
Yale Summers	Jack Dane (1966–1968)
Hedley Mattingly	Hedley
Hari Rhodes	Mike
Ross Hagen	Bart Jason (1968–1969)

Judy helps Clarence with his grooming. (*Archive Photos/MGM-TV*)

Erin Moran . . . . Jenny Jones
(1968–1969)
Clarence . . . . Clarence the
Cross-Eyed Lion
Judy . . . . Judy

Adventures Behind the Scenes

Judy was raised with affection training at Africa, USA, an animal compound located outside of Los Angeles and run by animal trainer Ralph Helfer in partnership with film and television producer Ivan Tors of *Flipper* fame. With the affection lavished upon Judy, she grew to be friendly and playful with an insatiable curiosity about the world around her.

Judy was permitted to stay in her trainer's home and sometimes to sleep in Helfer's bed. Her favorite spot was at the bottom of the bed, snuggled under the covers. Helfer dressed her in old baby clothes but did not have to worry about changing diapers during the night. Judy was toilet trained. On her own, she wiggled out from under the blankets, headed down the hall to the bathroom, turned on the light, closed the door, took care of business, unrolled toilet paper, flushed the toilet, turned on the faucet to wash her hands, dried her hands, turned off the light, and returned to bed, slipping quietly beneath the blankets.

Judy understood 75 different hand signals that cued her behaviors. Among her *Daktari* stunts were riding elephants, leading Clarence the lion on a leash, and engaging in pillow fights with that same cross-eyed critter. Despite a natural fear of reptiles, Judy even learned to become comfortable handling snakes. What a pro!

Judy was highly intelligent, and according to producer Ivan Tors, "Once she learned something, she utilized her knowledge." Judy absorbed filmmaking techniques and knew that an actor's exact physical actions must be repeated for close-up shots and for shots taken from different angles. She also learned that a loud whistle signaled the lunch break. When the whistle blew an hour later to signal a return to work, Judy resumed her exact position in the exact scene that she had left prior to lunch.

Notable Tidbits

For her work in *Daktari*, Judy won a PATSY Award in 1967.

Real Name: Pal

Breed: Collie

Star Qualities: Personality. One Hollywood critic called Lassie "a Greer Garson with fur." Pal was intelligent, brave, loyal, compassionate, and loving, and these star qualities shone brightly through his entire body of film and television work.

Special Tricks: In addition to the usual repertoire of canine tricks, Pal could crawl, act like a lame dog, act exhausted, open a door, take a person's hand in his mouth and guide the person to another location, climb a ladder, take a tumble, and hold his tail still.

Most Famous Role: Lassie in *Lassie Come Home* (MGM, 1943)

Plot

Needing money to sustain his impoverished Yorkshire family, a father sells his son's beautiful collie, Lassie. The new owner takes the dog to Scotland, but the dog escapes and begins a long journey fraught with dangers back to Yorkshire. Surviving the ordeal through the kindness of strangers, an exhausted Lassie is reunited with her young master and is allowed to come home for good.

Cast

Roddy McDowall	Joe Carraclough
Donald Crisp	Sam Carraclough
Dame May Whitty	Dolly
Edmund Gwenn	Rowlie
Nigel Bruce	Duke of Rudling
Elsa Lanchester	Mrs. Carraclough
Elizabeth Taylor	Priscilla
Pal	Lassie

Adventures Behind the Scenes

The character of Lassie was the brain child of Eric Knight, a newspaperman for the *Philadelphia Ledger*, who published a short story called "Lassie Come Home" in a 1938 issue of *The Saturday Evening Post*. Knight modeled Lassie after his own loyal, devoted dog, Toots. The story of Lassie caused such an emotional stir within the magazine's readership that Knight expanded the plot and published the story as a novella in 1939, selling more than one million copies. Subsequently, Metro-Goldwyn-Mayer acquired all theatrical rights to *Lassie Come Home* from Knight for $8,000.

As a boy, Rudd Weatherwax had an affinity for animals nurtured by life on a New Mexico ranch where his father used collies to control his herd of Angora goats. The elder Weatherwax passed along to his sons, Rudd, Frank, Jack, and Mac, his natural way of working with animals. After the family moved to Los Angeles in 1917, Rudd found a fox terrier looking for a home, adopted him, and taught him some basic dog tricks. Rudd and his dog hung around movie studios, hoping to be selected for extra work. One time Rudd was chosen to be a telegram delivery boy, and for the scene he had his dog hold the telegram in his mouth. This led to other small parts in films until Weatherwax was spotted by professional dog trainer Henry East, who gave him a job training dogs. Weatherwax learned the business from East from 1923 to 1940, training dogs such as Asta in *The Thin Man* film series and Daisy in the *Blondie* film series. "In 1940 my brother [Frank] and I opened our own kennel and school. Shortly after we opened, a man brought us an eight-month-old collie named Pal," Weatherwax said.

The man with the rambunctious puppy complained that the dog chased motor vehicles, chewed up everything in the house, barked incessantly, and refused to be housebroken. "Do you think you can train him for us?" the man asked. Rudd set about the task, and within a

Lassie and Roddy McDowall in 1943's *Lassie Come Home*. (*Archive Photos*)

week the dog was trained. When Rudd notified the owner that he could claim the dog, the owner balked. Having enjoyed a week's worth of peace and quiet, the man decided to keep the family collie-free. A deal was struck by which Rudd kept the collie in lieu of the training bill. From having worked with Pal for only a week, Weatherwax sensed that he was an extraordinary dog. So Weatherwax began training Pal for a potential movie career, and within six months, Pal had mastered twenty-five training lessons. "None of the other beginners could keep up with Pal," Weatherwax said.

When Pal was eighteen months old, a friend offered Weatherwax the chance to let his collie get away from it all at the friend's ranch. Because no movie work was on the horizon, Weatherwax allowed his friend to take Pal to the ranch. Weatherwax imagined his collie romping in meadows, chasing rabbits and birds, and having the time of his life. Several days into the dog's vacation, Weatherwax read a newspaper notice that Metro-Goldwyn-Mayer was looking for a strikingly beautiful collie to cast in an upcoming motion picture. Auditions

Lassie and Rudd Weatherwax. (*Courtesy of Frank Inn*)

would be held the following day. When Weatherwax went to claim Pal, the trainer was shocked. The dog's luxurious coat had been ruined by burrs from the underbrush as he had enjoyed his bucolic idyll. Weatherwax picked out hundreds of burrs, gave the dog a bath, and readied him as best he could for the afternoon audition. "I think he was the least striking of the three hundred and more collies who had come from all over southern California for the tryout," Weatherwax said. The production team completely bypassed Pal at the audition.

Because roles for collies were few and far between, Weatherwax was disappointed that Pal had blown a big chance. Weatherwax increased his grooming and training efforts with the dog, and six months later, when he heard that MGM still had not cast a collie for the picture, he took Pal (with coat now fully restored) to the Culver City studio for an audition that would show the collie's true talents.

"By this time, the movie people must have been growing desperate, because Pal and I were escorted immediately to the office of director Fred M. Wilcox," Weatherwax said. Pal trotted over to Wilcox and introduced himself by extending his paw. The director was enchanted. Weatherwax demonstrated Pal's talents, and Wilcox decided to have the pair meet the producer, Samuel Marx. After meeting Pal and seeing him perform, Marx invited Weatherwax to bring the collie back the following day for a film test. The film test showed that Pal photographed well, and the collie was offered a contract for the picture *Lassie Come Home*. But he wasn't selected for the lead. The studio was looking for a pedigreed female collie for the lead, and that part would go subsequently to another dog. Pal, a male without documentation of lineage, was chosen to be a double.

The San Joaquin River in northern California flooded, giving director Wilcox an opportunity to film the sequence depicting Lassie's struggle swimming the Tweed River separating England and Scotland. "Our feeling was all wet collies look alike. We figured we could match long shots of Pal with close-ups of the dog we had picked [to play Lassie]," Wilcox said.

Two cameras were used for the river scene, one in a boat about 50 feet from shore, the other on a low bank about 25 feet from the water's edge. Weatherwax and Pal sat in another boat in the middle of the water, awaiting a signal from Wilcox. At the signal, Weatherwax cued Pal to jump into the water. He swam by the camera boat and onward toward the designated spot on shore. In the meantime, the boat bearing Weatherwax rushed to shore so that the trainer could position himself behind the camera on the riverbank. "As he climbed out of the water and I signaled my commands to him, he put his tail between his legs, his head down, and slunk up the bank looking tired to the point of exhaustion," Weatherwax said. "Dropping down directly in front of the camera, he placed his head on the ground between his outstretched paws and slowly closed his eyes." Director Wilcox was astounded. Later, he told Weatherwax: "Pal jumped into that river, but it was Lassie who climbed out."

Pal was given the lead-dog role in *Lassie Come Home*. In the contract covering the estimated three-month production period, Pal was guaranteed a salary of $250 per week. Young Elizabeth Taylor, who played Priscilla, received only $100 per week for her work in *Lassie Come Home*—the same amount received by Pal's double dog.

"His training of the dog was phenomenal because the dog was absolutely amazing, stunning," Roddy McDowall said. "He was very good with his animals and very good as to how the animals related to the people with whom they had to work." Weatherwax allowed Pal to stay overnight with McDowall to allow the human and canine actors to bond.

Near the end of *Lassie Come Home*, McDowall, as the young Joe, leaves his schoolhouse and is startled to see his beloved but bedraggled Lassie waiting for him beneath a tree. The scene's action called for McDowall to rush to Pal and hug him as the collie licks his face. Pal's action was enhanced by ice cream smeared on McDowall's face so that the dog would lick him.

Weatherwax had to teach Pal to hold his tail still. "When the still cameraman took pictures of him on the film sets, the photos often would be blurred by a wagging tail," Weatherwax said. Pal was so happy to be working that his tail would just wag away; however, a bit of training soon produced the required result.

When *Lassie Come Home* debuted, dog lovers everywhere wrote letters of complaint to the studio, upset that Lassie had been allowed to climb the rocky seashore and suffer from bleeding feet. The studio calmed the irate viewers by explaining that tomato catsup had been used to simulate blood.

Lassie Come Home was among the ten best pictures of the year, and Pal went on to star in other Lassie adventures: *Son of Lassie* (1945), *Courage of Lassie* (1946), *Hills of Home* (1948), *The Sun Comes Up* (1949), *Challenge to Lassie* (1949), *The Painted Hills* (1951).

Memorable Movie Moment

Lassie swimming the swollen river and climbing exhausted onto the riverbank.

Notable Tidbits

Son of Lassie continued the story of Joe Carraclough, now an adult, and Laddie, Lassie's son. The female lead was played by June Lockhart, who later played Timmy's mother in the Lassie television series. One scene in *Son of Lassie* required Pal to tug on Lockhart's skirt until the skirt fell to the ground. Pal's incentive to perform this bit of acting? Pieces of meat sewn into the hem of Lockhart's skirt.

As Pal and other cast members of *Son of Lassie* returned to Hollywood by train from location filming in Canada, a young boy on the train followed Pal here and there during the excursion to Hollywood. When the boy saw Pal greet Peter Lawford, the lad approached the actor, asking, "Do you know Lassie?" Lawford responded: "Yes, I work with Lassie almost every day." The boy thought a moment and then asked, "Golly, how much d'ya have to pay to get to do that?"

Pal and Weatherwax reported for location filming at North Hollywood Park for a scene in *Son of Lassie* in which Laddie goes through an Army obstacle course. Several hundred children crowded the movie location, trying to catch a glimpse of the collie. According to Weatherwax, Pal was a ham in front of an audience, so the trainer allowed him to meet and greet the children. Weatherwax left Pal with his circle of fans for a moment, but when he returned he found that several boys were clipping locks of Lassie's hair. "Another half-hour and Lassie would have been a hairless collie!" Weatherwax said. The trainer convinced the kids to be content with patting Pal's head instead.

In addition to being a film star, Pal had his own radio show in the late 1940s. His weekly national broadcasts of *The Lassie Show* featured a dramatic dog story with Pal providing the required barks, growls, and whines.

Pal made personal appearances throughout the country, attracting huge crowds of fans. He had his own private plane so that he could be transported easily from film location to personal appearance site. When Pal traveled by train, it was strictly first class in his own private compartment.

The Lassie films required location filming, and by his fifth year of making motion pictures, Pal had logged about 20,000 travel miles. Personal provisions of water and food for Pal were shipped to each film location site.

Pal earned more than $200,000 for his work in the seven Lassie feature films and millions for Metro-Goldwyn-Mayer. But by the 1950s, MGM decided to drop its option on

Lassie. Because the studio still owed Weatherwax nearly $40,000, the trainer offered to cancel the debt if MGM returned to him all rights to Lassie. The studio agreed.

In late 1953, Weatherwax was approached about a television series for Lassie. Pal's son, called Lassie, shot a pilot film for the series, and the Campbell Soup Company immediately agreed to sponsor the half-hour weekly series. The first *Lassie* series was broadcast on CBS on Sunday night beginning September 12, 1954, with Tommy Rettig as Jeff Miller, Jan Clayton as his widowed mother Ellen, George Cleveland as Jeff's grandfather George "Gramps" Miller, and Donald Keller as Jeff's friend Sylvester "Porky" Brockway, all living in a rural community called Calverton.

Lassie was an instant hit, and the series garnered a number of awards during 1954, including an Emmy Award for Best Children's Program. The following year *Lassie* captured the Emmy Award again as well as the prestigious Peabody Award.

A number of cast and location changes occurred during the nearly 20

(*Courtesy of Frank Inn*)

years of the *Lassie* television series. In September 1957, Lassie became Timmy's collie. The Millers sell the farm to a childless couple, Paul and Ruth Martin, played by Jon Shepodd and Cloris Leachman, and Jeff Miller gives the collie to a seven-year-old orphan named Timmy (Jon Provost). In September 1958, the roles of Timmy's parents were played by June Lockhart and Hugh Reilly. By 1964 little Jon Provost had grown to adolescence, so the show's producers gave Lassie a new master, U.S. Forest Ranger Corey Stuart (played by Robert Bray). These *Lassie* adventures were filmed in color. Ranger Stuart was injured in a forest fire in the fall of 1968, and from then through 1970 Lassie was assigned to two young rangers, Scott Turner (played by Jed Allan) and Bob Erickson (played by Jack De Mave), although the collie roamed independently through many of the episodes. From fall 1971 through fall 1974, *Lassie* remained in production but was syndicated to television stations across the country. The last two seasons found a new family for Lassie, the Holdens, on a ranch in California. The role of Lassie throughout the various series was always played by descendants of the original Pal.

Acting as a stand-in for Lassie almost cost one double dog and the stuntman for Jon

Provost their lives. In the episode, Whitey Hughes and the double dog were on the Sonora River on a raft that was supposed to overturn in the rapids. Hughes had been warned of a dangerous crevasse filled with swirling water that could hold them down. Hughes fashioned a leather thong that he secured to the dog. "We went into that hole, it whirled us around, and we got disoriented. I could feel the dog trying to find his way on the wall, and I was trying to help him. When we hit the bottom of it, the dog was struggling and clawing at the wall, and I knew I was going to run out of air quickly. I gave a push and the dog began climbing, and when we hit the surface I just sucked in air. It would have been a lungful of water if we hadn't reached the top." Later when the dog was examined, Hughes discovered that he had torn off all the nails on his back feet from clawing and struggling in the crevasse.

Lassie won nine PATSY Awards from 1958 to 1971. In 1973, Lassie was inducted in to the Hall of Fame. In December 1975, *Esquire* magazine named Lassie among its collection of "Great American Things." Other honorees included Fred Astaire, Walter Cronkite, Marilyn Monroe, Jackie Robinson, and John Wayne.

Lassie became an animated cartoon in *Lassie's Rescue Rangers*, a Saturday-morning feature that ran on the ABC television network from 1973 to 1975.

A brand-new feature film debuted in 1978. *The Magic of Lassie* featured James Stewart, Mickey Rooney, Alice Faye, Mike Mazurki, Stephanie Zimbalist, and Pernell Roberts in a plot that updated and Americanized the story of *Lassie Come Home*. The Lassie who starred in *The Magic of Lassie* was a two-and-a-half-year-old sixth generation descendant of the original Pal.

MARCEL

Real Name: Monkey/Katie

Species: Capuchin monkey

Star Qualities: Ambitious. The two female monkeys who shared the role of Marcel, Ross Geller's quirky pet, "really like to work," according to Benay Karp of Benay's Bird and Animal Rentals, the company that trained and provided the pair. "Katie is very social and a little bit more affectionate, and Monkey does a little bit more of the harder stuff," Karp said.

Special Tricks: The monkeys are versatile. According to Karp, they can be trained for almost any behavior called for by a director. Their usual monkeyshines include going to their designated marks for a scene; carrying, catching, and throwing objects; and scampering to co-stars.

Most Famous Role: Marcel in the television series *Friends* (NBC, debuted in 1994)

(*Courtesy of Benay's Bird & Animal Source*)

Story Line

Six single, twentysomething friends residing in New York City share their lives, loves, hopes, and dreams while gathering at each other's apartments and in a Greenwich Village coffee cafe, Central Perk.

Cast

Jennifer Aniston	Rachel Green
Courteney Cox	Monica Geller
Lisa Kudrow	Phoebe Buffay
Matt LeBlanc	Joey Tribbiani
Matthew Perry	Chandler Bing
David Schwimmer	Ross Geller
Monkey/Katie	Marcel

Adventures Behind the Scenes

For each *Friends* episode, Monkey and Katie worked for five days to learn the tricks and stunts. "Some things were more difficult than others, and we utilized every day. We'd get two or three days to prepare, and then we'd block and shoot," Karp said. Monkey and Katie were cued by voice and hand signals.

"They work for treats and verbal praise," Karp said. Their favorite treat is a mealworm, the larva of various beetles; grapes are their next-favorite treat. But they don't work for peanuts; Monkey pulled down a cool $350 per day.

The character Marcel has been featured in a number of *Friends* episodes. "The One with the Monkey," broadcast in 1994, introduced Marcel as the pet that Ross adopts to cope with his post-divorce doldrums. Ross' friend rescued Marcel from an animal-testing lab. Soon Ross is further depressed when Marcel wrecks Monica's kitchen and begins to act out in other ways, such as by urinating on Monica's coffee table.

In "The One with the Stoned Guy," broadcast in February 1995, Ross is told that Marcel will help when Ross dates a museum curator. Instead, Marcel causes problems by leaping on the woman and hanging from her hair.

"The One with Two Parts—Part I and II," also broadcast in February 1995, shows Marcel causing problems for Ross, including pushing the wrong button on the television remote control and forcing the friends to watch an episode of *Laverne and Shirley* in Spanish. In Part II, Marcel swallows a K tile from a Scrabble game and Ross must rush him to the hospital.

In "The One with all the Poker," broadcast in March 1995, Marcel can't stop playing the song "The Lion Sleeps Tonight." In "The One Where the Monkey Gets Away," broadcast in March 1995, Rachel loses Marcel, who is almost captured by an animal control officer. In "The One With the Fake Monica," broadcast in April 1995, Marcel begins "loving" everything he sees, and Ross learns that he must give up his pet.

According to Karp, the most challenging episode for Monkey and Katie was "The One after the Superbowl—Part I and II" broadcast in January 1996. It was difficult because of the additional number of cast members (Chris Isaak, Julia Roberts, Brooke Shields, Jean-Claude Van Damme, Fred Willard, etc.), the amount of monkey action required, and the presence of other animals. In that episode Ross learns that Marcel is dead, then discovers that not only is Marcel alive, but he is the Monkey Shine Beer Monkey and the star of *Outbreak II*. Ross reunites with his former pet, then says good-bye to Marcel.

Monkey had a role in a Diet Coke commercial with the cast of the Emmy-nominated *Friends*. Television, film, and commercial work—Monkey and Katie do it all.

Monkey was close to actor Matt LeBlanc, who plays Joey. Unfortunately, Monkey and David Schwimmer were more like oil and water. In fact, Schwimmer stated, "I hate the monkey. I wish it were dead." According to Benay Karp, "Apparently, he didn't like the monkey, but we liked him." Shortly after Schwimmer's statements broke in the press, Marcel was written off the program. But according to Karp, Marcel can always be called back, and Monkey and Katie would be thrilled to return to their *Friends*.

Notable Tidbits

In 1995, Monkey branched out into film work, playing the pivotal role of the monkey infected with a killer virus in the biomedical disaster thriller, *Outbreak*. To get the contagion ball rolling, Monkey, who had been stolen from an animal-quarantine facility, spit water on the abductor, and the *Motaba* virus was off and running. During filming, three other capuchin monkeys acted as stand-ins.

MATISSE

Real Name: Mike
Breed: Border collie
Star Qualities: Striking features. Mike is black and white with one brown and one blue eye.
Special Tricks: Mike's repertoire of tricks included more than 300 behaviors. Mike's most spectacular stunt was climbing a rope ladder while holding a pail of water in his mouth.
Most Famous Role: Matisse in *Down and Out in Beverly Hills* (Touchstone Pictures, 1986)

Plot

A wealthy businessman saves a homeless man from drowning, invites the unfortunate man to move into his Beverly Hills estate, then watches as the man takes over the neurotic lives of the household's members.

Cast

Nick Nolte	Jerry Baskin
Richard Dreyfuss	Dave Whiteman
Bette Midler	Barbara Whiteman
Tracy Nelson	Jenny Whiteman
Evan Richards	Max Whiteman
Elizabeth Pena	Carmen
Little Richard	Orvis Goodnight
Donald F. Muhich	Dr. Von Zimmer
Mike	Matisse

Adventures Behind the Scenes

To win the role of Matisse, Mike performed a routine of tricks for director Paul Mazursky during the audition. Mike's owner/trainer Clint Rowe pulled a special one out of Mike's bag of different tricks and expressions—climbing a rope ladder while holding a pail of water in his mouth. Mazursky was blown away by Mike's antics but was seeking a smaller dog. Four weeks later, after auditioning a kennel of compact canines, Mazursky changed his mind and decided that the part belonged to Mike.

Mike and Rowe worked together for five weeks training for *Down and Out in Beverly Hills*. Dog and trainer spent ten weeks shooting the movie, to which director Mazursky added a number of scenes to showcase Mike's talent. Mike's rewards for performing included his favorite food nibble, broiled chicken breast.

Mike the Dog presents a PATSY award with Carmelita Pope, former director of the Los Angeles office of the American Humane Association. (*Courtesy of the American Humane Association*)

One stunt that Mike did not perform was the leap into the swimming pool. That was performed by Mike's double, Davy.

Mike and Nick Nolte worked well together during filming, but according to Rowe, "Little Richard was scared to death of the dog." Rowe thinks that aversion might have developed when Mike and Davy were introduced to the stars. "They usually never fought, but Little Richard was a little unsure, and as he put his hand out I said, 'It's okay; they're real gentle,' and all of a sudden, Davy grabbed Mike. And it wasn't bad, but they made a lot of noise. Little Richard screamed, and he jumped on top of the piano bench," Rowe said. Later, Mike and the piano-pounding singer made up with a hand shake on *The Tonight Show*, and Mike graciously appeared in Little Richard's music video for the theme song to *Down and Out in Beverly Hills*, "Great Gosh A'mighty."

Memorable Movie Moment

Matisse has refused to eat for the last three days, so Barbara Whiteman summons canine psychiatrist Dr. Von Zimmer for an emergency house call. In soothing tones, the good doctor greets his patient and offers him a bowl of doggie nuggets. Matisse grabs the bowl with his teeth and flips the contents all over the room.

"Oh, Matisse. Oh, Matisse. You're very angry, aren't you?" Dr. Von Zimmer thinks that Matisse is disturbed because of the houseguest, Jerry Baskin, and because of the hostility that Dave Whiteman shows toward the dog.

"What this dog needs is love and reassurance. And he needs love and reassurance from you," the doctor tells Dave. "You must go and caress this dog. And hold him. Hug him. Give him some affection."

"Oh come on! The dog is running the whole house," Dave yells.

Dr. Von Zimmer badgers Dave about Matisse's delicate psychological state until Dave reluctantly gets down on his knees and gives Matisse a hug. "Nice dog, nice dog, you're a very nice dog," Dave tells Matisse.

While dog and master bond, Dr. Von Zimmer speaks privately to Mrs. Whiteman. "When your guest leaves, Matisse will eat. He'll be voracious. He'll be okay. I wouldn't worry about that. But he has other problems. I believe he suffers from nipple anxiety. Probably came from a nine-dog litter. Now about my fee . . . "

Notable Tidbits

On his way to Washington State, Clint Rowe discovered Mike tied to a dog house on a sheep farm in northern California. Although Rowe was interested in the border collie, the owner didn't want to sell the five-month-old puppy, so Rowe drove on. One hundred miles later, Rowe stopped, telephoned the owner, and asked again to buy the dog, indicating that he would drive back to the farm that day to pick up the pup. Impressed with Rowe's sincerity and willingness to return, the owner agreed to the sale.

Before breaking into the motion picture business, Mike was an actor in television commercials. Following *Down and Out in Beverly Hills*, Mike appeared in other films, a children's song video, and soft drink and dog food commercials.

The critics raved about Mike's performance as Matisse. *USA Today* proclaimed him "the most lovable screen animal in years." The *New York Times* declared that "Mike does Oscar-caliber work," while the *Chicago Sun-Times* stated that "Mike, the dog, should get an honorary walk-on at the Oscars." Mike did appear on the animal-equivalent of the Academy Awards—he served as co-host of the 1986 PATSY Award ceremony.

Real Name: Bamboo Harvester

Breed: Golden Palomino

Star Qualities: One-Take Wonder. Bamboo Harvester was extremely bright. He could learn a scene in fifteen minutes, and with the cameras rolling perform the scene flawlessly in one take. He could also respond to commands of twenty to twenty-five words from his trainer Les Hilton.

Special Tricks: Bamboo Harvester was able to unlatch a stable door, open a file cabinet drawer, write notes, pick up coins, dial a telephone.

Most Famous Role: Mister Ed in the television series Mister Ed (CBS, 1961–1966)

Story Line

Architect Wilbur Post and his wife Carol escape city life by buying a Connecticut country home that boasts a stable within which lives a horse named Mister Ed. To Wilbur's surprise, he discovers that Mister Ed is a talking horse that will speak only to him. Episodes concerned Wilbur's struggles and misadventures as he tries to conceal from his wife, his neighbors, and others that he owns a talking horse.

Cast

Alan Young	Wilbur Post
Connie Hines	Carol Post
Larry Keating (1961–1963)	Roger Addison
Edna Skinner (1961–1963)	Kay Addison
Jack Albertson (1963–1965)	Paul Fenton
Leon Ames (1963–1965)	Gordon Kirkwood
Florence MacMichael	Winnie Kirkwood
Richard Deacon	Dr. Bruce Gordon
Rocky Lane	Voice of Mr. Ed
Bamboo Harvester	Mister Ed

Adventures Behind the Scenes

The idea of a talking horse and the name Mister Ed originated in a series of magazine short stories by Walter Brooks. Arthur Lubin, who had directed the movies featuring Francis the Talking Mule thought that television was ripe for the misadventures of a talking horse. In 1957, Lubin took an option on the Mister Ed concept and the following year obtained $75,000 in financial backing from comedian George Burns to produce a pilot. The episode was shot using Scott McKay and Sandra White as the leads and a horse other than Bamboo Harvester as Mister Ed. However, none of the networks was interested in the series.

The pilot eventually caught the attention of Al Simon, president of Filmways TV Productions. Although Simon found many production flaws, he thought the pilot's premise had the potential for high hilarity. The Mister Ed concept was resurrected, and a three-minute sales film was shot with a new cast, featuring Alan Young, Connie Hines, and a second horse in the role of Mister Ed. The Studebaker Corporation agreed to sponsor the show in syndication. *Mister Ed* debuted in January 1961, became a smash hit, and was picked up by CBS for their fall 1961 Sunday lineup. When the show premiered on October 1, 1961, Mister Ed became network television's first non-cartoon talking animal.

Trainer Les Hilton found Bamboo Harvester, the horse that starred in the series, on a farm in the San Fernando Valley. Hilton liked the palomino because "he had the right kind of eyes, and he sure was sensitive." Bamboo Harvester was the sire of Chief Tonganozie (a half Arabian) and Zetna (an Arabian). Full grown, he was 15 hands high and weighed 1,100

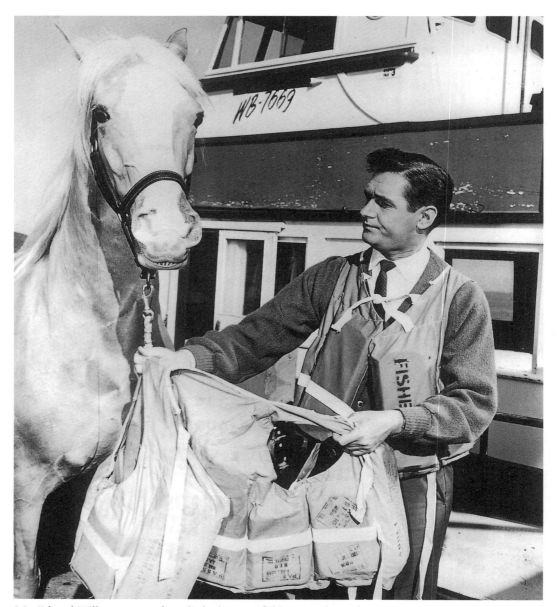

Mr. Ed and Wilbur prepare for a little deep sea fishing. (*Archive Photos*)

pounds. Bamboo Harvester's grandfather, named The Harvester, was famous for strutting his stuff in the Rose Bowl Parade. Filmways purchased Bamboo Harvester for $1,500.

Bamboo Harvester put in a long day on the Mister Ed set. He and his trainer Les Hilton (who also trained Francis the Talking Mule and Flicka) arrived on the set at 7:30 a.m., and the horse was back in his stable by 6 p.m. Every day Bamboo Harvester downed 20 pounds of hay and a gallon of sweet tea. Hilton rewarded the horse with an occasional carrot for work well done.

Bamboo Harvester did not rely on his stand-in, Punkin, for his stunts such as opening the door to the stable or dialing the telephone. He did all the work himself with his trainer cueing the behaviors with hand signals or voice commands. Mister Ed's most amazing behavior was moving his lips to "talk." How this behavior was accomplished had been kept super secret by the show's producers. However, Whitey Hughes, a horse stunt man and friend of Les Hilton, revealed for the first time how Hilton achieved this clever effect. The horse's bridle was fashioned with a nylon fish line which fed into his mouth. When Hilton pulled the line, the horse tried to dislodge it by moving his lips. Thus, Mister Ed appeared to talk.

Who provided the voice of Mister Ed? The identity of that individual was kept top secret for years, too. The deep, baritone voice of Mister Ed belonged to Allan "Rocky" Lane, one of the most popular movie cowpokes in the late forties and early fifties. Lane and his horse, Black Jack, galloped through 38 westerns for Republic Pictures, and Lane was twice ranked among the top 10 Western moneymakers. He replaced Wild Bill Elliott in the Red Ryder series, played that comic strip cowboy in seven films, then obtained his own "Rocky" Lane series of films. Nicknamed "America's fightin'est cowboy," Lane fell on hard times after the B Western faded into the sunset in 1954. Minor parts here and there barely kept him afloat until he auditioned for and won the role of providing the voice of Mister Ed.

The beginning of the show featured the stable door opening and Mister Ed announcing, "Hello, I'm Mister Ed." This line led to the program's theme song, composed by Jay Livingston and Ray Evans, that began "A horse is a horse, of course, of course." The first six episodes of *Mister Ed* featured the music but not the lyrics because the producers couldn't find the right singer. Originally, the theme had been recorded by an Italian opera singer, but this rendition turned out to be a disaster. The producers had liked the demo version of the song that Jay Livingston had sung for them and asked Livingston to provide the vocals temporarily until a professional singer could be found. Livingston's version worked so well—he even deep-voiced the line "I am Mister Ed" at the end of the song—that the producers gave up their search for a singer and used Livingston's version of the theme for the episodes.

The fact that Mister Ed wore an enormous pair of eyeglasses for reading was part of the show's shtick and resulted from a stroke of serendipity. While taking a walk, associate producer Herb Browar found the novelty lenses in a shop on Hollywood Boulevard and brought them to the studio the next day. As a joke, someone suggested that the glasses were just the right size for Mister Ed, and voila, a "sight" gag was born.

The sight of Mister Ed sliding to home plate in the episode "Leo Durocher Meets Mister Ed" had many fans scratching their heads in amazement. How did Mister Ed do that? The scene involved not Bamboo Harvester but a fake stuffed horse to which the special-effects man had attached a length of bungee rubber. With one end secured at home plate, the other end that was attached to the horse was stretched tightly up the third-base line and secured. At the right moment, the rubber was cut and the horse was pulled, dust and all, across home plate.

In "Ed the Stowaway," Mister Ed had the chance to "hang ten" in Hawaii. For this scene, trainer Les Hilton helped Bamboo Harvester become accustomed to standing on a large surfboard, director of photography Arch Dalzell used the rear-projection process to make it seem as if Mister Ed was riding the waves, while a special-effects team splashed water on him.

Notable Tidbits

In his off-screen hours over the years, Bamboo Harvester made a number of special appearances. He visited the Children's Hospital in Los Angeles, allowing the small fry patients to touch him and to sit on his back. He appeared in a 19-minute short feature in 1964 called "Wilbur Gets the Message" to promote payroll savings bonds. In the film, Mister Ed uses the telephone to order savings bonds in Wilbur's name. In 1966, after track officials rejected Mister Ed's entry in the five-furlong race the "Astronaut Stakes," Bamboo Harvester picketed the Hollywood Park Race Track as a publicity stunt. He wore sandwich boards proclaiming: "Hollywood Park Unfair to Showbiz Horses!" and "I've Been Rejected As A Racehorse!"

Bamboo Harvester didn't horse around when it came to winning PATSY (Performing Animal Top Stars of the Year) Awards. He won an award every year from 1962 through 1965.

Bamboo Harvester went to that Big Stable in the sky in 1968, but news of his demise was not announced at the time because the series was still being shown around the country. Eleven years later, newspapers carried the story that Mister Ed died on February 28, 1979 in Oklahoma. This horse, owned by Hollywood animal trainer Clarence Tharp, was actually a Mister Ed lookalike. Was this palomino the first horse used in the Mister Ed pilot episode? Was this horse used by Filmways merely for Mister Ed publicity poses? No one is certain, but the newspaper stories coupled with the lack of publicity surrounding the passing of Bamboo Harvester years before led many fans to believe erroneously that the horse in Oklahoma had been the real Mister Ed.

MURRAY

Real Name: Maui

Breed: Collie mix (part border collie, part collie)

Star Qualities: Spoiled rotten. According to Maui's owner, Boone Narr of Boone's Animals for Hollywood, Maui has his own air-conditioned dressing room, a personal telephone line, and a couch for relaxing between scenes. When he makes personal appearances, he flies first class and has access to a chauffeured limousine. "He doesn't know what it is like to be in a dog crate anymore," Narr said. "He gets a little uppity sometimes, but his Mom, Bingo, straightens him out."

Special Tricks: "Maui is very sweet and takes direction well," according to his trainer, Betty Linn. "Maui is definitely smarter than Murray, and he knows tons of tricks." Maui's specialties are "hiking" or making people think he is relieving himself, sneezing, crawling, shaking his head, and rolling over. He also enjoys chasing an invisible mouse.

Most Famous Role: Murray in the television series *Mad About You* (NBC, debuted in 1992)

(© *TriStar Television. Courtesy of Columbia TriStar Television*)

Story Line

Paul and Jamie Buchman are a young, urban couple trying to maintain their marital bliss through the challenges of love in the 1990s.

Cast

Paul Reiser . . . . Paul Buchman
Helen Hunt . . . . Jamie Buchman
Anne Ramsey. . . . . Lisa Stemple
John Pankow. . . . . Ira Buchman
Leila Kenzle . . . . Fran Devanow
Richard Kind. . . . . Mark Devanow
Maui. . . . . Murray

Adventures Behind the Scenes

Boone Narr discovered Maui in an animal shelter in Castaic, California along with his mother, Bingo. Bingo starred in the 1991 film *Bingo*, and Maui served as his mother's double.

When the call came to audition dogs for the role of Murray, Narr brought 25 dogs to show to the program's creators, Danny Jacobson and Paul Reiser. "Paul picked the dog that he felt would be good for the show, but it was not Maui," Narr said. "It was another dog that I felt at the time was the wrong dog, but Paul just had his eye on this dog." The show began rehearsals, and according to Narr, Reiser and the dog did not have a good rapport. "The dog was miscast for that role. He just didn't seem to fit the family or Paul, and the dog actually growled at Paul one day," Narr said. So Reiser decided to replace the dog and called for another round of animal auditions. "Both Maui and his mother Bingo went up for the part, and Maui was picked," Narr said. "Since Bingo is Maui's double dog, it works great because if Maui came down with a cold and couldn't work then his mother could fill in for him." In fact, Bingo is Maui's only double.

According to Narr, Maui fits well with the main characters on *Mad About You*. "Maui's personality goes along with Paul's and Helen's," Narr said. "He's laid back. He's a family dog. Instead of doing fancy tricks, most of the time you'll find him laid out on the couch, on the floor, on the bed with them, and he's just there just like anyone's dog would be. He blends with Paul and Helen so well. They love him."

Maui as the lovable but dense Murray has been featured in a number of episodes. In the second season's opener, "Murray's Tale," Jamie's sister Lisa takes Murray out for a walk but returns with a dog named Simon that clearly isn't Murray. Maui played the dual roles of Murray and Simon. In 1994's "The Last Scampi," Murray meets his mother, Mona (played by Maui's real-life mother Bingo), and the Buchmans learn that Murray used to be named Swifty. In the third season, "Just My Dog" relates the tale of Murray's show-business career, which begins with a walk-on appearance in a commercial directed by Paul, is advanced by Bob the eager agent, and culminates in an audition for a series. "Just My Dog" allowed

Maui to meet Jay Leno and to be hugged by Rachel Hunter. In the fourth season, "An Angel for Murray" finds the Buchman's hiring a professional dog walker, Nat, to walk Murray—who seems to prefer the professional over Paul.

"Every show we let Maui go up into and meet the audience in between the takes so they can pet and greet and say hi to him. He loves that," Narr said. Maui receives hundreds of fan letters a week. Fans also send him presents. Past gifts have included a doggie bed and bubble-gum machine that dispenses dog biscuits with the flick of a dog-bone-shaped lever.

Maui is finicky when it comes to food rewards, according to Narr. "I think his favorite is roast white meat chicken breast with no skin—he won't eat dark meat—flavored with just a little bit of garlic," Narr said.

According to Narr, there's no special lady in Maui's life. "Just his Mom. He's real close to his mother," Narr said. "They've always been together. When he's not working, he plays with other animals, but he really likes to play with his mother."

Notable Tidbits

In the summer of 1994, Maui shared the cover of *TV Guide* with Moose (Eddie, the canine star of *Frasier*). In fact, Maui captured the cover of *TV Guide* before either Paul Reiser or Helen Hunt. Maui was voted the most popular dog on television.

According to Narr, Maui has won the American Kennel Club Award, was voted an honorary American Kennel Club canine ambassador to promote well-trained dogs, and has completed walkathons with Brooke Shields in New York City to promote AIDS awareness.

Thanks in part to Maui, *Mad About You* was named Outstanding Comedy Series in 1994 by Viewers for Quality Television. The series was nominated for an Emmy Award in 1994. In 1995 the series was honored with a Golden Globe award as Best Series, Musical, or Comedy, as well as with the prestigious Peabody Award for excellence in television.

PETE THE PUP

Real Name: Pete

Breed: American Pit bull terrier

Star Qualities: "Pete was a pussycat," according to Tommy Bond who portrayed Butch in the Our Gang comedies. The gang mauled him, grabbed his ears, and rode him like a horse, but Pete never snapped, growled, or bit.

Special Tricks: Whenever trouble loomed, Pete would lie down, place his paws over his head, and close his eyes.

Most Famous Role: Pete the Pup in Our Gang comedies from 1927 to 1938, including *The Pooch* (#115) (MGM, 1932)

Plot of <u>The Pooch</u>

Stymie rescues the gang's dogs from the dog catcher. When the dog catcher discovers what Stymie has done, the mean man retaliates by snatching Stymie's dog, Pete the Pup. He threatens to put Pete to sleep unless Stymie brings five dollars to the dog pound. Stymie prays for help, receives a windblown five-dollar bill, and rushes to the pound to save Pete. The dog catcher tells Stymie that he's too late, but Pete pops up and takes off after the dog catcher.

Cast

Matthew Beard, Jr.	Stymie
George McFarland	Spanky
Dorothy DeBorba	Echo
Kendall McComas	Breezy Brisbane
Sherwood V. Bailey, Jr.	Spud
Harold Wertz	Bouncy
Robert Hutchins	Wheezer
Budd Fine	Dogcatcher
Pete	Pete the Pup

Adventures Behind the Scenes

In 1927, producer Hal Roach was looking for a new mascot for his Our Gang comedies. The dogs he had been using lacked personality and had a limited repertoire of tricks. Roach auditioned at least fifty dogs, including Pete, who was the son of the bulldog Pal, the first dog to appear in early Our Gang movies. Pete had a role in 1925's *The Freshman* (Pathe) with Harold Lloyd, and he had played Tige in the early Buster Brown comedies. Roach was impressed with Pete's training and experience but didn't like the ring around his eye. That's when Roach learned that the ring had been applied with a permanent liquid dye when Pete had the role of Tige. The ring that the producer didn't like and couldn't be removed soon became Pete's famous trademark.

Pete was signed to a three-year contract with six-month options. He earned a starting salary of $125 a week which was raised by $25 increments to $225 during the period of the contract. The contract also gave Pete an extra $25 per week to ensure that his services were exclusive to Hal Roach Studios.

The original Pete was owned and trained by dog breeder Harry Lucenay. In fact, Pete's contract with the studio stated that if Lucenay trained another dog who performed better than Pete, the new dog would step into the role. At least three and perhaps up to a dozen dogs played Pete in the Our Gang comedies.

In *The Glorious Fourth* (#64) released in 1927 and *Playin' Hookey* (#65) released in 1928, Pete's character was named Pansy. In subsequent films, he was known as Pete the Pup.

With numerous dogs playing the role of Pete, the striking ring around the eye had to be recreated. Hal Roach remembered that "we just painted the ring around whichever eye would show it off the best." But sometimes for a retake or insert shot, the ring was applied

(*Movie Star News*)

to the wrong eye by mistake. When Roach caught the goof, he had the film lab reverse the shot so that the ring would appear correctly. At other times, the goof went undetected. For example, in *The Pooch* (#115) the ring is around Pete's left eye. In 1934's *Hi'-Neighbor* (#126), the ring is around Pete's right eye.

Pete had a lead role in 1927's *Dog Heaven* (#70). This two-reeler was a novelty not only because the story was told through Pete's eyes, but because of its a grim story line. In the film, Pete thinks that his longtime master Joe Cobb has abandoned him to spend time and money on a flirtatious girl. Despondent, Pete finds comfort in a bottle of booze. Joe finds him drunk and berates poor Pete. When Joe's girlfriend is pushed into a lake by another dog, Pete rescues her but is accused of causing her near drowning. Joe is disgusted with Pete, so the broken-hearted pup decides to end it all by hanging himself. Pete prepares a noose, says a prayer before slipping it around his neck, but is stopped at the last moment by Joe and the gang. A tearful Joe explains that he now knows that another dog actually pushed his girl into

the lake and that Pete is actually a hero. Joe and Pete make up. The pair are happy once again, and Joe gives Pete a brand new collar.

Pete appeared in both group shots with the gang and in specialty shots that highlighted his unique acting talents such as putting his paws together in "prayer." The specialty shots were filmed separately, usually while the gang was in school. Pete and his trainer worked together to perfect the trick, then the camera rolled to capture a tight shot of Pete in action. The specialty shot was then inserted with group scenes during the editing process.

Rehearsing for the 1932 comedy *Spanky* (#113) was a painful experience for Pete. The script called for three-year-old Spanky McFarland to hit a rubber bug with a hammer, but the propman, Don Sanstrom had attached a concealed wire to the bug. Each time Spanky tried to hit the bug, Sanstrom pulled it away. Pete watched the gag repeated several times. Frustrated, Spanky took another whack at the bug, missed the mark, and hit Pete's foot. With a yelp, the pup took off and hid under a bed.

Following *The Pooch* in 1932, Pete's owner was terminated by the studio. The regular studio trainer, Tony Campanero, then trained replacement pit bulls for the role of Pete. The new dogs were unrelated to Pete but continued the name. Campanero also ran the ranch producer Hal Roach maintained as a home for all the animals used in his films, including the new Petes.

Notable Tidbits

Each year Pete accompanied members of the gang on personal appearances at charity events across the country. A member of the audience during a 1934 appearance in Atlantic City, New Jersey, was a boy named Fred Rogers. Years later, Rogers donned a cardigan sweater and became the star of television's *Mr. Rogers' Neighborhood*. In remembering his meeting with the perky pit bull, Rogers said "I certainly liked sitting with Pete."

The single-reeler *Bored of Education* captured an Academy Award as the Best Short of 1936. *Bored of Education* concerned the unhappiness of Our Gang at the prospect of returning to school after a long summer vacation. Spanky and Alfalfa concoct a scheme to get out of class but are outwitted by their clever teacher. The short featured George "Spanky" McFarland, Carl "Alfalfa" Switzer, Eugene "Porky" Lee, Billie "Buckwheat" Thomas, Darla Hood, and Pete the Pup.

Pete the Pup won new generations of fans when the Our Gang films were brought to television in the 1950s as *The Little Rascals*.

Former Our Gang actor Jackie Cooper also has fond memories of Pete. "I loved that dog," Cooper wrote in his 1981 autobiography. Cooper felt that staying a whole weekend with the Our Gang dog was his "idea of glory and paradise combined."

Pete the Pup returned to the modern silver screen in 1994 in the feature film, *The Little Rascals*, which featured Travis Tedford as Spanky, Bug Hall as Alfalfa, Brittany Ashton Holmes as Darla, Zachary Mabry as Porky, Ross Bagley as Buckwheat, Sam Saletta as Butch, and a new-generation Pete the Pup played by an adorable pit bull with a ring around his eye.

Real Name: King Charles
Breed: Thoroughbred
Star Qualities: Difficult. According to co-star Elizabeth Taylor, "He took a hunk out of the shoulder of the man who tried to train him to play dead for the film. Except for the jockey who did some of the jumps in the National, I was about the only person who could ride him—and bareback with just a rope around his neck."
Special Tricks: King Charles could jump over an automobile.
Most Notable Role: The Pie in *National Velvet* (MGM, 1944)

Plot

Young Velvet Brown, who has a passion for horses, dreams of a "breathtaking piece of folly"—training her spirited horse, The Pie, to qualify and run in the English Grand National

Steeplechase. She encourages her young horse-trainer friend, Mi Taylor, to train The Pie, then disguises herself as a jockey to run the race and cross the finish line.

Cast

Mickey Rooney	Mi Taylor
Elizabeth Taylor	Velvet Brown
Donald Crisp	Mr. Brown
Anne Revere	Mrs. Brown
Angela Lansbury	Edwina Brown
Juanita Quigley	Malvolia Brown
Jackie "Butch" Jenkins	Donald Brown
Reginald Owen	Farmer Ede
King Charles	The Pie

Adventures Behind the Scenes

Enid Bagnold's 1935 novel *National Velvet* featured a black-and-white piebald horse with large distinct patches. Bagnold had named Velvet's horse The Pie because of its distinctive markings. After MGM acquired the film rights to the novel, the name of the horse remained the same—The Pie—even though King Charles was a Thoroughbred. The name was explained in an early scene of the film when the original owner of the horse calls him Pirate.

King Charles was the grandson of the champion racehorse Man O'War. King Charles was purchased for *National Velvet* for $800.

Eleven-year-old Elizabeth Taylor undertook a rigorous training program to prepare for the part of The Pie's owner, Velvet Brown. Taylor took horseback-riding lessons and jumping instruction at the Riviera Country Club and at the Dupee Stables in Hollywood. Knowing that King Charles would be the horse used in the film, Taylor bonded with him, riding him for an hour and a half each day, feeding the horse, and leading him.

MGM's front office was horrified when it received news that Taylor was completing up to forty jumps a day on the spirited King Charles. Taylor was quick to come to the defense of the horse: "But he loves me," she said. "He wouldn't hurt me. You don't have to worry about King when you get on his back. You just leave everything up to him. I think that he likes to know that I leave it to him—that he's the boss, and I trust him."

The special bond that Taylor had with King Charles was evident to everyone on the set. While most gave him plenty of space because of the horse's tendency to bite, cast and crew were amazed to see Taylor walking on the back lot with King Charles following close behind her.

The scene in which The Pie is near death required Taylor to cry. Mickey Rooney offered acting advice, telling Taylor that she should imagine a series of family tragedies to bring her to tears: her alcoholic father dying, her mother forced to earn money by doing laundry, her brother without shoes, and her puppy killed by a car. According to Taylor, "When I did the scene, instead of imagining my father drunk and dying and my mother

Jackie Jenkins, Elizabeth Taylor, The Pie (King Charles), and Mickey Rooney in *National Velvet*.

(*Movie Star News*)

doing laundry in the snow, all I thought about was this horse being very sick, and that I was the little girl who owned him. And the tears came."

For the jump scenes and the steeplechase, stuntman Billy Cartlidge rode King Charles while Taylor watched from the sidelines. The horse threw him during filming, causing the stuntman to injure his back.

Memorable Movie Moment

Velvet and Mi decide that Ivan Taski, the jockey hired to ride The Pie in the Grand National, is not suitable. Velvet makes up her mind that she will be the one to ride The Pie in the race. In the trailer, she tells Mi that she will impersonate Taski during the race. Mi tries to talk her out of the notion, but he reluctantly agrees that she can ride. Velvet asks Mi to cut her hair, using The Pie's scissors, so that she will look like a boy. While clipping her locks, he warns her that she will be disqualified when the officials discover she is a girl; she will have to forfeit the prize money and maybe even go to jail for fraud. He then begins to coach her for the next day's race, but she stops him. Mi challenges her, "Do you think a race like this is won by luck?" "No. By knowing The Pie can win and telling him so."

Notable Tidbits

Elizabeth Taylor loved King Charles so much that during filming and after the Christmas 1944 debut of the film, she begged producer Pandro S. Berman to let her keep the horse. "I would give anything in the world if I could only get that horse," Taylor told Berman. Berman approached the head of the studio, Louis B. Mayer, who agreed to present Taylor with King Charles. "She was the happiest kid I ever saw," Berman recalled. Taylor received word on her thirteenth birthday that King Charles would be hers. Adolescent ardor for a beloved animal often matures years later to the reality of adult responsibility. In 1959, Berman was in a Manhattan restaurant when Taylor approached him. "Aren't you the guy who gave me King Charles after *National Velvet*?" she asked. When Berman replied, "Yes, I am afraid I am," Taylor glared at him with violet eyes and said: "You son of a bitch, do you know I'm still paying for feed for that goddamned nag."

The 1944 film became the basis for a 1960–1962 television series starring Lori Martin as Velvet, Arthur Space and Anne Doran as Mr. and Mrs. Brown, James McCallion as Mi Taylor, and a horse named King as The Pie. After the series ended, King was retired to a farm for underprivileged children on the outskirts of Cincinnati. The farm was owned by the Ohio hamburger chain, Frisch's Big Boy.

In 1978 a sequel to the story of Velvet Brown, *International Velvet*, starring Tatum O'Neal and Anthony Hopkins, featured the fictional last foal from Velvet's The Pie named Arizona Pie. The film faltered to mixed reviews.

QuIncy

Real Name: Isaac

Breed: Basset hound

Star Qualities: Method actor. Isaac could portray convincingly a fat, old, lazy dog because he was a fat, old, lazy dog.

Special Tricks: Isaac could sit and stay for long periods of time. "His trick was not moving even though there was banging and crashing noises on the set, sounds from the audience, and motion from the cameras. He could stay in position, put down his head, and not move," according to Cheryl Shawver of Animal Actors of Hollywood.

Most Famous Role: Quincy in the television series *Coach* (ABC, 1989–1997)

Story Line

Coach Hayden Fox strives for a winning season not only with his team but with his colleagues, friends, and family. Episodes related the touchdowns as well as the fumbles of Fox's life as an athletic coach.

Cast

Craig T. Nelson	Hayden Fox
Jerry Van Dyke	Luther Van Dam
Shelley Fabares	Christine Armstrong Fox
Bill Fagerbakke	Dauber Dybinski
Kenneth Kimmins	Howard Burleigh
Katherine Helmond	Doris Sherman
Isaac	Quincy

Adventures Behind the Scenes

A dog that no one wanted, Isaac was adopted from an animal shelter, trained to perform animal action, and worked in television—he had a recurring role in the NBC soap opera *Santa Barbara*—and in Purina commercials before becoming a prime-time TV star.

According to Cheryl Shawver, after the production team for *Coach* put out the call for a dog, they looked at a number of hounds. They weren't happy with any of the dogs they saw until they met Isaac, even though the other dogs were more highly skilled and trained than Isaac. "He wouldn't have been our first choice, but he was exactly what they were looking for," Shawver said. "He was the character Quincy. Instead of having to act the part, he was the part." The part of Quincy called for an old, fat, sweet basset hound, and according to Shawver, Isaac was "a lazy, not really brilliant dog" who at nine years of age had grown almost as wide as he was long.

"He learned new tricks for an episode, and then the writers would write them into the script," Shawver said. Isaac's main action was really no action at all. He was called upon to sit in a red wagon and stay in the wagon no matter what while being pulled around by his owner, Luther Van Dam (played by Jerry Van Dyke). According to Shawver, doing nothing isn't as easy as it looks. "To do nothing and do it in the right space and time made Isaac work as hard as if he was being made to do something complicated."

No double dogs for Isaac; he did all of the animal action himself. Memorable episodes included Quincy swallowing a Superbowl ring and having the characters wait for him to pass it and visiting a pedigreed dog and being arrested for breeding her.

"He was a lazy old boy, so he really wasn't into toys," Shawver said. Instead, Isaac's motivators included praise and food. His favorite foods included cooked chicken and turkey and commercial dog food. Treats for special occasions included bacon strips or pieces of beef or liver.

Although Isaac died in his sleep during the run of the series, the production team decided to continue his character. Another dog was used in his place. The new dog was lighter in color than Isaac had been, so the new dog had to be colored to match the late Isaac. The production team wrote Quincy's death into the story line. In that episode, a contingent of dogs appears at a eulogy to remember their friend, the characters recall their favorite Quincy memories, and Luther receives a new puppy decorated with a big red bow.

Notable Tidbits

Isaac may have been sweet and lovable, but he suffered the stigma of all hound dogs—body odor. Despite frequent baths and liberal applications of perfume, Isaac still smelled. Thankfully his winning personality more than made up for deficiencies in the area of personal hygiene.

RHUBARB

Real Name: Orangey (official name)
Breed: Red tabby American domestic shorthair
Star Qualities: Workaholic. Various Rhubarb cats have appeared in more than 500 television series and motion pictures.
Special Tricks: Rhubarb could snarl, jump, retrieve and carry objects, sit on a person's shoulders, climb a ladder, and walk a tightrope.
Most Famous Role: Rhubarb in *Rhubarb* (Paramount, 1951)

Plot

The eccentric owner of a seventh-place Brooklyn baseball team dies, leaving the club and his vast fortune to a snarling, spitting cat named Rhubarb. The cat becomes the lucky charm mascot of the team when the club begins to win games. When Rhubarb is catnapped by gamblers who want the team to lose the World Series, the cat's guardian and his highly allergic fiancée "sniff" out the catnappers.

Cast

Ray Milland	Eric Yaeger
Jan Sterling	Polly Sickles
Gene Lockhart	Thaddeus J. Banner
William Frawley	Len Sickles
Elsie Holmes	Myra Banner
Taylor Holmes	P. Duncan Munk
Orangey	Rhubarb

Adventures Behind the Scenes

Frank Inn was working for Rudd Weatherwax, the trainer of Lassie, when Paramount put out a call for cats for the role of the baseball-team-owning cat from H. Allen Smith's novel, *Rhubarb*. Cat work paid peanuts in comparison to dog work, and Inn usually got stuck with the task of finding a cat for a film then training the cat according to the script. "So whenever I'd go to the pound, I'd pick up two or three cats that looked alike, struggle through, and try to get the job done," Inn recalled. "But cats that were good, I would keep. Finally I had quite a few trained cats." Other animal supply companies borrowed Inn's cats for film roles from time to time, and if Inn was not busy training Lassie, he would work a cat for another company. Several trainers, including Henry East, Rudd Weatherwax, and Earl

Rhubarb and Frank Inn being interviewed about *Rhubarb*. (*Courtesy of Frank Inn*)

Johnson, borrowed a number of Inn's cats to show for the role of Rhubarb.

Arthur Lubin, the director of *Rhubarb*, had worked on a previous film with Inn. Lubin called Inn and requested that the trainer show his cats. Inn explained that his cats had already been auditioned by other trainers, but Lubin insisted that Inn show his cats himself. When Inn explained this situation to his boss, Weatherwax gave Inn the go-ahead. After all, Lassie wasn't scheduled to work immediately, and Inn would have plenty of free time. Because Weatherwax knew Inn would not make much money if he received a contract, he also told Inn that he could keep all the money from the work.

Inn had five days to prepare a few of his best-trained cats for the Paramount audition. When he showed his cats to the production team, Inn's cats climbed a ladder, jumped on the trainer's back, retrieved a ping-pong ball, lay on their sides, hissed and spit, and ran after him on cue. The production team was impressed with Inn's skills and the cats' abilities, so they sat down to discuss business. "They gave me a contract and more money than I had ever made working a dog because of the way I showed the cats," Inn said. "I went back to tell Weatherwax, and I didn't dare tell him how much I was getting." This was Inn's first independent training job, and he had 30 days to find a cat to train for *Rhubarb*.

As a publicity stunt, Paramount advertised for a cat to play the part of Rhubarb in the film. "People sent cats from all over the country," Inn said. "Paramount was stuck with cats. Many people brought their cats down to the studio, and many people wrote in about their cats." The production team looked at more than 500 cats and more than 3,000 photographs. The studio gave Inn the most promising leads, and he was charged with evaluating likely cat prospects.

One likely prospect was a homeless cat named Orangey befriended by a woman in Sherman Oaks, California. The woman wrote to the studio and enclosed a photograph of the animal. Her letter said that in 1948 a cat had wandered into her garden covered with cuts, scrapes, and bruises. She nursed him until he recovered, then tried to set him free, but he refused to leave. Inn visited the cat at the woman's home. Although the cat had the right look, he was so wild that he tore up the crate Inn had brought to transport him to the studio. Finally Inn captured the critter, paid the woman $25 for him, and brought him to the studio. Unfortunately, an illness swept through the caboodle of cats that Inn had amassed and because Orangey was a stray without proper inoculations, he died even before filming could begin. Paramount decided to keep the demise of Orangey a secret and to play up in the press the alley-cat-makes-good angle of the story.

Because cats are difficult to train, Inn was not sure he could teach one cat all of the tricks necessary for the *Rhubarb* script. Instead, he acquired 60 look-alike cats and used 36 of them for the film. Inn trained each of the 36 cats to perform one or two tricks and used the cats interchangeably in the film. For example, when the director needed a cat to jump, Inn brought out one of the cats that could jump on cue. The cat would perform the trick, Inn would put the cat back in its crate and take out another that could perform the next trick requested by the director.

The *Rhubarb* script called for the cat to spit. To gain realism, Inn brought a dog to the studio and cued the dog to bark at the cat. When the dog barked, the cat raised its back and spit on cue.

For one scene, Rhubarb had to affectionately lick Ray Milland's hand. Inn accomplished this by smearing the actor's hand with liver paste.

Inn had various names for the 36 cats with which he worked—Pie Plant (another term for Rhubarb), Big Boy, Long Tail, The 'Fraidy Cat, Little Britches. However, the official press releases from the studio promoted the story that one cat, Orangey, played the role of Rhubarb.

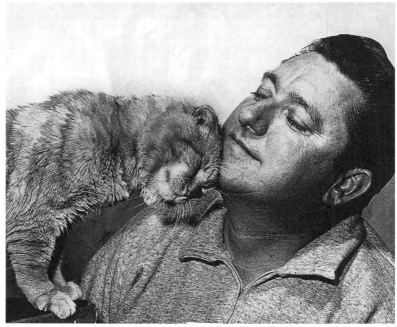

Rhubarb shows Frank Inn a lovable side. (*Courtesy of Frank Inn*)

According to Inn, The 'Fraidy Cat was a fearful animal. "It was so scared that if I set it down, it would run to its crate," Inn said. "He became a good cat to run down the street. All I had to do was set his crate down, toss a piece of meat in, carry him down the sidewalk. When I turned him loose, he just ran like the dickens to get to his crate. And he just stayed in there."

Memorable Movie Moment

Slipping out of his collar and chain, Rhubarb outwits Pencil Louie's henchman, who is guarding him in the hotel room. The cat jumps through the door's open transom and hot foots it down the hall just as Eric and Polly arrive. Eric grabs Rhubarb, and the trio rushes to street level to catch a cab and speed away. They don't get far because a car containing Pencil Louie and his goons forces the cab to the side of the street. Rhubarb escapes from the cab, streaking through Manhattan streets toward the ball park. As he makes his way to Brooklyn, residents speed him along. Rhubarb arrives at Banner Field, climbs the vine-covered wall surrounding the stadium, lands on the field, and rushes to the owner's box. The team is ecstatic at his return and wins the World Series.

Notable Tidbits

Frank Inn's *Rhubarb* cats made appearances in more than 500 television programs and feature films. A *Rhubarb* cat appeared as Minerva on *Our Miss Brooks* from 1952 to 1956 and on *The Beverly Hillbillies* as the swimming cat. Film work included *Breakfast at Tiffany's* (1961) as Cat [winner of the 1962 PATSY Award]; *The Incredible Shrinking Man* (1957); *The Diary of Anne Frank* (1959); *Gigot* (1962); *True Grit* (1969); and others. According to Inn, anytime a dog chased a cat in a television show or motion picture, the animal was probably a *Rhubarb* cat.

Rhubarb won the 1952 PATSY Award. Rudd Weatherwax, whose dog Lassie had yet to win a PATSY, expressed his frustration to Inn: "Frank, you *know* that cat isn't smarter than Lassie."

While Inn was doing the animal action on *The Beverly Hillbillies*, he made a $5 bet with a photographer that he could teach a cat to swim. Inn worked with one of the *Rhubarb* cats to effect this amazing behavior. He dug a small circular trench on his property and filled it with about an inch of water. He placed some food a little beyond the trench then called the cat, which jumped over the trench to reach the food and then jumped back. Inn dug the trench wider and wider until the cat could no longer span the trench in a single leap. Instead, the cat landed in 18-inches of water and swam to the end of the trench to retrieve the food. Inn collected the bet from the astonished photographer, who then spread the word around the studio about the incredible swimming cat. The production team on *The Beverly Hillbillies* was amazed as well and wrote the cat into the story line. "That cat learned to stand on the edge of a pool and swim to the other side," Inn said. On the series, the swimming cat was called Rusty and was one of the many critters of Elly May (played by Donna Douglas).

RIN TIN TIN

Real Name: Golden Boy, Jr., nicknamed J.R.

Breed: German shepherd

Star Qualities: Quick learner. According to Rand Brooks, who played Corporal Boone on the television series *The Adventures of Rin Tin Tin*, "The dog was just unbelievable. He only had to be shown once what you wanted and he did it."

Special Tricks: J.R. could go to a file cabinet, open a drawer, remove an object from the drawer, and bring it to his handler.

Most Famous Role: Rin Tin Tin in the television series *The Adventures of Rin Tin Tin* (ABC, 1954–1959)

Story Line

In the 1880s, a United States cavalry troop discovers the only survivors of a wagon train attacked by Indians: a young boy, Rusty, and his faithful companion, Rin Tin Tin. The pair is brought to Fort Apache to await their relocation. Rusty and Rin Tin Tin save the life of a visiting colonel, and as their reward, Rusty is made a honorary soldier, and Rin Tin Tin becomes the troop's mascot. Episodes related the involvement of Rusty and Rin Tin Tin in the life of the Fort, including battles with marauding Indians and gun-slinging Western villains.

Cast

Lee Aaker	Rusty
James Brown	Lt. Rip Masters
Joe Sawyer	Sgt. Biff O'Hara
Rand Brooks	Cpl. Boone
J.R.	Rin Tin Tin

Adventures Behind the Scenes

The Rin Tin Tin dynasty had its beginnings in Fleury, France, on September 13, 1918, during the last days of World War I. While on patrol, American Air Force pilot Lee Duncan stumbled upon a bombed-out building that had served as a kennel for German war dogs. In a trench near the building, Duncan found a mother German shepherd and her six puppies, whimpering and shaking in the cold. He brought the dogs back to his base, where all were adopted. Duncan chose a male pup that he christened Rin Tin Tin and a female pup that he called Nanette, naming them after the lovers in a French legend. According to the legend, the lovers and 40 others scrambled for the safety of a railroad station during a German air attack. During the bombing, the station was destroyed, and the only survivors were Rin Tin

Lee Aaker and Rin Tin Tin (J.R.)

Tin and Nanette. Duncan returned to the United States with the puppies after the war, but Nanette died from pneumonia shortly after her arrival.

As a dog lover, Duncan enjoyed showing the surviving dog, whom he nicknamed Rinty, at dog shows. But during one show, a reviewer commented on Rinty's clumsiness, and this criticism spurred Duncan to begin training his dog. Duncan worked with Rinty in a narrow hallway to avoid interruptions that would break the dog's concentration. The trainer used a shoe to teach the fetching behavior and threw the shoe only short distances to simulate the working area on a movie set. With time and patience, Duncan trained Rinty to not only sit and fetch but to perform hundreds of tricks, and soon Rin Tin Tin was ready for Hollywood.

Hollywood wasn't ready for Rin Tin Tin until 1923 when Warner Bros.—a studio teetering on the brink of bankruptcy—featured the dog in the silent adventure film *Where the North Begins*. Audiences loved Rin Tin Tin and flocked to theaters to see him tangle with villains. So popular was Rin Tin Tin that revenue from his films single handedly saved Warner Bros. from financial collapse, and he became known as the dog that saved Hollywood. (Rin Tin Tin's story was satirized in the 1976 film *Won Ton Ton: the Dog Who Saved Hollywood*.) Rinty enjoyed a nine-year film career, appearing in movies such as *Tracked by the Police* (1927), *Hills of Kentucky* (1927)—which introduced Rin Tin Tin, Jr.—and *The Man Hunter* (1930). His last film was *The Lightning Warrior* in 1931. United Press announced Rinty's death on August 10, 1932 with this notice: "Rin Tin Tin, greatest of animal motion-picture actors, pursued a ghostly villain in a canine happy-hunting grounds today."

Rin Tin Tin, Jr., or Rinty II, followed in his father's famous paw prints starring in *The Pride of the Legion* (1932), *The Big Pay-Off* (1933), *Tough Guy* (1936), *The Silver Trail* (1937), *Skull and Crown* (1938). Rinty II's career ended by 1938 when his popularity declined, and new film offers dried up.

By early 1947, Lee Duncan had trained the grandson of the original Rinty—Rin Tin Tin III. Rinty III was a World War II K-9 Corps veteran, having held the rank of sergeant. He had been awarded a Purple Heart for an injury sustained when a jeep ran over his leg during maneuvers. Rinty III knew more than 500 commands for tricks such as pretending to sleep, scratching fleas, ringing a bell, and stalking prey by creeping on his belly. Duncan was ready to introduce the dog to Hollywood and get back to making movies. But he feared that because Rinty had been off the scene for so many years, movie audiences would not remember him. Duncan commissioned a survey, which showed that 95 percent of the respondents were familiar with the famous dog and wanted to see him star in another film. The film, *The Return of Rin Tin Tin*, opened in the fall of 1947 and starred Rinty III, Bobby (Robert) Blake, Donald Woods, and Claudia Drake. Although the picture did well at the box office, no sequel was made.

In the early 1950s, the television subsidiary of Columbia Pictures, Screen Gems, contacted Lee Duncan about bringing Rin Tin Tin to television in *The Adventures of Rin Tin Tin*. Duncan was retired at this time but was willing to work with the current member of the Rin Tin Tin dynasty. Unfortunately, Duncan found that he was not up to the pace of training Rinty for the weekly television series.

Another German shepherd trainer, Frank Barnes, and his dog Golden Boy, Jr., were brought onto the series. Golden Boy, Jr.—nicknamed J.R.—was the son of Flame, a dog that

The original Rin Tin Tin in *Tracked by the Police* (1927).
(*Museum of Modern Art/Film Stills Archive*)

had appeared in the *Rusty* series of films during the 1940s. J.R. appeared in *The Adventures of Rin Tin Tin*, which debuted on October 15, 1954, and had a successful run of 164 black-and-white episodes. The cry "Yo ho, Rinty!" brought J.R. running throughout the series.

Barnes used a combination of voice and hand signals to work J.R. and the other dogs used in *The Adventures of Rin Tin Tin*. Quiet, friendly J.R. was the main dog for close-up work. He was not allowed to engage in fighting action, so his stand-in, named Hey You, worked the fight scenes. J.R.'s other double was named Bearheart, and he was used in long shots.

Although J.R. was protected from interaction with the other animals on the set, his friendly nature proved his undoing on one occasion. The scene required J.R. to take a lariat off the horn of a saddle and bring it to actor James Brown, who played Lt. Rip Masters. As J.R. took the rope in his mouth, the horse turned his head to look at J.R. "He walked over and gave the horse a big slurp, and the horse bolted around and kicked him," Brown remembered. "It didn't hurt him too bad, but he limped around for a couple of weeks, and we had to shoot scenes around him until he was feeling better." After that incident, double dogs were used for horse action scenes.

Notable Tidbits

From 1930 to 1934, Rin Tin Tin and then Rin Tin Tin, Jr., performed on a weekly radio adventure program. Listeners heard Rinty, billed as the "Wonder Dog," corner and catch radio crooks.

Actor James Brown and J.R. performed at rodeos and fairs to promote *The Adventures of Rin Tin Tin*. One crowd-pleasing routine involved Brown asking Rinty, "What happened when you got your foot caught in that bear trap?" J.R. would then limp around the stage.

Then Brown would ask: "Was it that foot or the other one?" J.R. would then switch feet and limp with the other one.

J.R. won PATSY Awards for his portrayal of Rin Tin Tin in 1958 and 1959.

SALTY

Real Name: Tiki

Breed: Himalayan cat

Star Qualities: Star attitude. According to trainer Tammy Maples of Jungle Exotics, Tiki and her Himalayan stand-ins were trained to respond to a buzzer. "The other cats run to the buzzer whenever they hear it for their food, and Tiki comes, but she always walks. There is never any running. Her attitude is 'Well, you can wait for me.'"

Special Tricks: Tiki sits and stays for up to 45 minutes at a time. "She has an incredible atten-

Tiki and Lea Thompson in *Caroline in the City. (Courtesy of The Lippin Group)*

tion span. I think that's what makes her so different from other cats. Nothing fazes her. People can fall in front of her, and she'll still stay there," Maples said.

Most Famous Role: Salty in the television series *Caroline in the City* (NBC, debuted 1995)

Story Line

Cartoonist Caroline Duffy mines Manhattan for love, happiness, and raw material for her weekly comic strip. She finds inspiration in her personal life with its various romantic disasters and in the lives of her colorist Richard and her best friend and neighbor Annie. Other sources of material include her boss Del, president of the greeting card company that features her "Caroline" cards, and the company's adrenaline-propelled go-fer Charlie.

Cast

Lea Thompson . . . . Caroline Duffy
Eric Lutes . . . . Del Cassidy
Malcolm Gets . . . . Richard Karinsky
Amy Pietz . . . . Annie Spidaro
Andy Lauer . . . . Charlie
Tiki . . . . Salty

Adventures Behind the Scenes

Tiki was adopted by Tammy Maples of the California firm Jungle Exotics when the breeder who owned Tiki could no longer use her for breeding. Tiki had lived in a cage all of her life, had never been outside, and had never lived in a house. When she came to live with Maples, terrified Tiki stayed under a bed for four months, coming out only at night to eat.

As Tiki became adjusted to her new surroundings, she gradually spent less time under the bed and more time getting acquainted with Maples. Still shy, Tiki became the office mascot because Maples did not think she could transform the hyper Himalayan into a working animal. "When they were looking for animals for *Homeward Bound: The Incredible Journey*, the producers came into the office and saw her sitting there. They said, 'We don't know what we're casting for the dogs, but we know that that's Sassy right there.' So we had to start working with her," Maples said. "They liked her looks and her attitude. She had the same attitude that Sassy in the movie had."

To prepare Tiki for her acting debut, Maples first had to get the cat accustomed to the sights, sounds, and smells of the outdoors. Maples worked with Tiki for three months to prepare her for the film work; the filming itself took sixty days. "The turnaround she did was amazing," Maples said. "The time and the effort that we put into her just made her blossom. She really enjoyed the attention she got when she was working."

For *Homeward Bound: The Incredible Journey* (1993), Tiki was the lead or close-up cat. "She had to learn to work with the dogs," Maples said. "The bulldog puppy was such a boisterous little guy, she and the other cats learned that if they stuck with the golden retriever, they'd be safe from the puppy's pounces."

Tiki had seven stand-ins for *Homeward Bound: The Incredible Journey*. After the film, some of the stand-ins were adopted as pets, but three of the hardest workers—Remington, Curly, and Chubby—became Tiki's stand-ins on *Caroline in the City*. The stand-ins also act to keep Tiki and her star attitude in line. If Tiki doesn't want to perform, Maples brings out a stand-in, and Tiki quickly hits her mark. "She doesn't want to see another cat get rewarded," Maples said.

According to Maples, Tiki's role on *Caroline in the City* is to irritate people (especially the character Richard) and to just be herself. In some episodes, Tiki had an expanded role. For example, in one episode when Caroline was ill, she stuck a note to Salty's tail and sent her downstairs to get ginger ale. Another time, Salty was knocked out of a window and had to be taken to the vet. In the second season, the story line introduced a Salty shaken by all of the changes taking place in Caroline's life. "The turmoil caused Salty to start misbehaving, so a cat therapist was called in," Maples said.

"She enjoys being on the set," Maples said. "She makes herself at home in the apartment, she knows her spots and her places, and she recognizes the cast and crew pretty well. The only problem we've had is that she purrs while she's working. She'll be really happy while she's sitting there, she's warm under the lights, and she'll start purring, and the sound people come down and say, 'We can hear her purring.'"

Tiki's motivators include food and affection. "She's a real picky eater, and her favorite food is chicken," Maples said. "But she only likes white meat, and she prefers canned chicken not the kind cooked at home. She will accept an occasional cat treat. She also will do some of her behaviors just for my stroking her."

Cast members like and interact with Tiki on the set. Lea Thompson has owned cats for years, and since Tiki plays her cat on the program, Thompson handles the Himalayan very well. Amy Pietz talks and plays with Tiki, even though her character doesn't have much interaction with Salty on the series. "They all have quiet time with her," Maples said. That includes actor Malcolm Gets who, as the character Richard, views Salty as his *bête noire*.

"Malcolm hates to do anything antagonistic to her on the show because he's gotten so much hate mail from doing it," Maples said. Maples recalled one scene in which Richard found Salty shedding her long hair on his black coat. The action called for him to shoo her off, and the actor balked, asking if Tiki could be called off instead. "Malcolm is really worried about people thinking that he hates the cat when he really is very good with her," Maples said.

Notable Tidbits

According to Maples, Tiki's relationship with the exuberant bulldog on *Homeward Bound: The Incredible Journey* evolved from her hiding by the golden retriever to asserting herself. "When they were all running together, if she got ahead of the bulldog at all, he decided that she was fair game to chase," Maples said. "So she'd turn around and have to give him a couple of whacks on the nose. They used some of that in the movie." In the film, Sassy's voice was dubbed by Sally Field.

In *Homeward Bound: The Incredible Journey*, Tiki was too special to perform the scene in which the character Sassy falls into the swiftly flowing river. That action was done by her stunt doubles Remington and Curly.

SCRUFFY

Real Name: Scruffy

Breed: Mixed wire fox terrier

Star Qualities: Strong willingness and deep desire to do anything for his trainer, Karl Lewis Miller, as long as Scruffy received a toy as his reward.

Special Tricks: Running, jumping, retrieving, padding with his paws, grabbing an ankle and holding on tenaciously.

Most Famous Role: Scruffy in the television series *The Ghost and Mrs. Muir* (NBC, 1968–1969; ABC, 1969–1970)

Story Line

After the death of her husband, freelance writer Carolyn Muir moves her family—a son, daughter, housekeeper, and pet dog—to Schooner Bay in New England. Renting charming Gull Cottage from the current owner Claymore Gregg seems to be a fine way for Mrs. Muir to make a fresh start except that the ghost of the previous owner, Captain Daniel Gregg, a nineteenth-century sea captain, is determined to scare off the new occupants. Episodes related Mrs. Muir's efforts to transform the cottage into a home, the protests of the Captain who longs for his privacy, their eventual truce, and the fondness they developed for each other.

Cast

Hope Lange	Mrs. Carolyn Muir
Edward Mulhare	Captain Daniel Gregg
Reta Shaw	Martha Grant
Kellie Flanagan	Candice Muir
Harlen Carraher	Jonathan Muir
Charles Nelson Reilly	Claymore Gregg
Scruffy	Scruffy

Adventures Behind the Scenes

The television series was based on the 1947 movie *The Ghost and Mrs. Muir*, starring Gene Tierney, Rex Harrison, and Natalie Wood. In the film, the family pet was a cairn terrier named Rusty.

Two weeks before the casting call came for a dog to play Rusty in the television series, trainer Karl Lewis Miller dropped by the animal shelter in North Hollywood. "I saw in the back of one kennel a little furry ball just hanging back and being intimidated by the other dogs," Miller remembered. To gain the little dog's attention, Miller shooed away the other dogs that crowded the front of the enclosure. This lured the little dog to Miller and allowed the trainer to play with him through the wire of the cage, give him doggie treats, and see the dog's frisky nature emerge. The dog had been at the shelter for nearly two weeks and was scheduled to be put to sleep in two days if no one claimed him. At the time, Miller had no need for a new dog and no room for an addition to the brood of animals he already had. But two days later, Miller returned to the shelter and, because the little dog remained unclaimed, adopted him.

When the casting call for *The Ghost and Mrs. Muir* came, Miller and his then-boss Lou Schumacher brought a variety of canines to the studio to show to the producer, Gene Reynolds. None of the dogs they had shown in three separate auditions had the personality or the look that Reynolds was seeking. "As we were all done with the interview, we could see the disappointment in Gene's face that we still had not found the dog," Miller said. By chance, Miller had brought the little dog from the shelter along for the ride to the third audition, and the dog was waiting in the car. Schumacher suggested that Miller show Reynolds the little dog since the pooch had a different look from the other dogs they had shown. "The dog was untrained," Miller said. "He had a different attitude from any calm, well-behaved dog. As I brought him in, he was tugging and straining on the leash, tangling the leash in my feet, uncontrollably jumping up on the coffee table, going up and sniffing people's crotches. Gene looked at the dog and said 'That's him! That's Rusty. That's the attitude I want in the dog,' which completely blew our minds." Reynolds had been looking for a dog that acted not like a trained dog but like a real dog. Miller's job became to train the little dog from the shelter for the pilot episode of the series.

"The dog had no name at this time because I had had him for only two weeks, and I was trying to think of the right name for this dog," Miller said. When Miller received the pilot's script, he scanned the descriptions of each character. "Rusty's description was 'the sassiest, scruffiest, most nuisance dog in the world and yet lovable,' and out of that description I found the word "scruffiest," and decided to call this dog Scruffy."

Miller had four weeks—a shorter time period than he would have liked to have had—to train Scruffy for the role of Rusty, using basic obedience training. "This dog really at first took offense to it," Miller said. "He always acted browbeaten, not that he was, but it was against his wishes to become humanized." Numerous times Scruffy escaped from his training session to hide under a bed, snapping at Miller's fingers when the trainer reached in to retrieve him. "He was just a problem student," Miller said. "But whenever I got into a problem and thought I might be losing my patience or losing his interest, lucky for me, he was a fox terrier. He was really toy and ball crazy. He'd do anything to play with a toy or ball. So I used toys in the training to make it pleasurable for him or to at least keep his interest in me. And literally for the pilot episode, we skated through that not with a trained dog but with a toy-crazy dog because I tricked him into doing everything in the script with a toy." When the script called for Rusty to run up the stairs after the ghost, Miller tossed a ball up the stairs and the dog would run up the stairs. For the title shot, which called for Rusty to walk along the beach with Mrs. Muir's son, Miller put a squeaky toy under the armpit of young actor Harlen Carraher. As the boy walked, he flapped his arms, squeaking the toy. The dog pranced on the beach, looking up at the boy hoping to get the toy. When Rusty had to attack the owner of the cottage, Miller put a squeaky toy in actor Charles Nelson Riley's sock. "The dog would just latch onto that toy on his ankle and not let go," Miller said.

After the pilot sold and the series went into production, Miller continued training Scruffy. "By this time, the dog was so bonded with us that he accepted training well," Miller said. Miller taught Scruffy one trick a week. The trick was then incorporated into that week's script.

After several weeks of hard training, on the first day that Miller and Scruffy reported to work at the Twentieth Century-Fox studio, Scruffy had a reluctant-child-going-to-school attitude. With his tail tucked down and his ears bent back, Scruffy strained against the leash until they entered the stage area. There they were greeted by shouts of joy from the young actors playing Mrs. Muir's children, Kellie Flanagan and Harlen Carraher. "As they ran toward the dog, Scruffy's tail started wagging; his ears perked up; he started bouncing on the leash trying to get to the kids. That was the turning point. All of a sudden Scruffy was delighted to be working," Miller said.

During scene rehearsals, young Harlen confused the character's name with the dog's name even though Miller gently pointed out time and time again that the boy needed to call the dog Rusty rather than Scruffy. "At one point, I think out of frustration, Gene Reynolds decided to make it simple for the child and suggested calling the dog Scruffy in the show. So the show carried the dog's real name," Miller said.

Scruffy got along well with all the cast members, but because of their frequent on-screen interactions, his biggest relationship was with Charles Nelson Riley. "Charles, the professional that he is, did whatever he could to have the dog relate to him," Miller said. Charles allowed Miller to have Scruffy practice jumping on his lap, barking at him, padding on his pant's cuff. "Charles would go along with whatever it took for me to get this dog to respond to him," Miller said.

Notable Tidbits

After *The Ghost and Mrs. Muir* ended in 1970, Miller had a difficult time securing other acting roles for Scruffy. "He was typecast, and he lost work for about three years. At every casting call, every time we showed him, nobody wanted him because he was recognizable as Mrs. Muir's dog," Miller said.

Scruffy's break came after a casting call was issued for a well-trained dog to be featured in an episode of the television detective drama, *Barnaby Jones*. Although Scruffy was immediately rejected at the first audition, Miller brought him back for a second audition. This time Miller "mangied him up and discolored his fur" so that Scruffy looked like a different dog. "They were quite interested in him," Miller said. "They wanted to see him do more and more tricks, and I just worked him. By this time—after two years of a TV series and another three years of time with this dog—Scruffy was the best trained dog I had ever had." The audition team thought so, too. In fact, even though the dog was a little darker than they wanted for the part, Scruffy won the role.

"It was two or three days into the shoot before I admitted that it was one of the dogs that they had rejected before," Miller said. The production team wasn't upset. This version of Scruffy had a unique look—a look they liked—and he had a certain attitude that was right on the mark. "I had him groomed in a different way, and I didn't present him as a cutsy dog from *The Ghost and Mrs. Muir*," Miller said, "and he started working left and right and non-stop for another two years." In addition to his work in the *Barnaby Jones* episode, Scruffy made appearances on *Kung Fu*; *The Rockford Files*; *The Streets of San Francisco*; *Love, American Style*; *Bracken's World*; *Happy Days*; *CHiPS*; *Mannix*; *Perry Mason*; and others.

In 1970, Scruffy won a PATSY Award for his performance in *The Ghost and Mrs. Muir* and a PATSY in 1974 for a Chuck Wagon Dog Food commercial. Scruffy was inducted into the Hall of Fame in 1977.

Real Name: Traveler

Breed: Traveler was a pure white, pink-skinned part Morgan and part Arabian

Star Qualities: Camera shy. Traveler hated the sound of the camera and showed his displeasure by refusing to obey the commands of his trainer. During scenes that did not require dialogue, the crew spoke loudly or made noise so that Traveler wouldn't hear the noise of the camera.

Special Tricks: Rearing up on his hind legs for the Lone Ranger's trademark line: "Hi Yo, Silver. Awa-a-a-y!"

Most Famous Role: Silver in the television series *The Lone Ranger* (ABC, 1949–1957)

Story Line

The Lone Ranger, a masked man with a white horse, and his faithful Indian companion Tonto right wrongs during the days of the Old West.

Cast

Clayton Moore	The Lone Ranger (1949–1952, 1954–1957)
John Hart	The Lone Ranger (1952–1954)
Jay Silverheels	Tonto
Traveler	Silver

Adventures Behind the Scenes

The Lone Ranger, Tonto, and Silver were characters developed for a local radio program called *The Lone Ranger*, which debuted on Detroit radio station WXYZ on January

30, 1933. To simulate Silver's hoof beats, sound engineers pounded bathroom plungers in a large box filled with gravel.

The creative team that developed the radio program wrote an unforgettable introduction for The Lone Ranger and Silver: "A fiery horse with the speed of light, a cloud of dust and a hearty 'Hi Yo, Silver!' The Lone Ranger." The "Hi Yo, Silver!" required extensive brainstorming. At first the team tried "Hi-Yi!" then "Yippee!" and other shouts that were not quite in keeping with the flavor they were seeking. In frustration, someone suggested using the British "Heigh-Ho." That was tried several times until it became slurred into "Hi-Yo," and the team finally had their Lone Ranger shout—"Hi-Yo, Silver!"

The Lone Ranger was christened "kemo sabe" by Tonto. Tonto told the Lone Ranger that the phrase meant "trusty scout." The original director of the radio program, James Jewell, knew no Indian words, so he created the phrase from the name of a Michigan boys' camp known as "Kee Mo Sah Bee"

For a radio theme, Jewell asked the record turner and sound effects assistant, Bert Djerkiss, to select a sample of dramatic recordings from the radio station's music library. Djerkiss auditioned close to thirty selections for Jewell to consider. Jewell narrowed the field to two: "March of the Light Brigade" and the "William Tell" overture. He chose the latter as the theme for The Lone Ranger because of its inspiring fanfare. Little did Jewell realize the impact his selection would have on the listening audience. Several months after The Lone Ranger began broadcasting, Leopold Stokowski conducted a symphony concert in the Westwood Gardens in Detroit. The opening selection was the "William Tell" overture. When the orchestra played the fanfare, Stokowski was dumbstruck when the entire audience responded with "Hi-Yo, Silver!"

Many of the radio scripts were written by Francis "Fran" Striker, a script writer from Buffalo, New York. Striker created the fictional origins of the Lone Ranger and Silver: A posse of Texas Rangers under the command of Captain Daniel Reid pursues a band of notorious outlaws led by Butch Cavendish. Ambushed in a canyon by the outlaws, the six Rangers fall in a rain of bullets. The outlaws ride away certain that all are dead. That night, an Indian comes upon the scene of the slaughter and discovers that one of the Rangers is still alive. The Indian cares for the Ranger until he regains consciousness. "You only Ranger left," the Indian says, "You lone Ranger now." The Indian, Tonto, and the Ranger had met years before when the Ranger—then a boy—had saved the Indian's life and became Tonto's "kemo sabe." The Ranger vows to avenge the deaths of the other Rangers by bringing the Cavendish gang to justice. He dons a black mask to hide his identify from the lawbreakers, and the Lone Ranger and Tonto hunt down all the gang members except the elusive Butch Cavendish.

While following Cavendish's trail, the Lone Ranger and Tonto are ambushed, and the Lone Ranger's horse falls dead. They head to Wild Horse Valley where the companions watch a legendary white stallion losing a battle with a fierce buffalo. As the buffalo prepares to make a final death charge at the fallen steed, the Lone Ranger rushes into the fray with guns drawn and shoots the buffalo. The Lone Ranger cares for the battered, bruised, and severely wounded stallion until the mighty horse recovers. Then the Lone Ranger attempts to put his saddle on the horse, but the animal breaks free and runs away. "Him look like silver," Tonto says. "Silver, that would be a name for him," the Lone Ranger agrees. He calls out

A stirring duo: Silver and the Lone Ranger. (*Archive Photos*)

(*Archive Photos*)

that name to the stallion, and the horse, at first hesitating, gallops back to him. After several days of bonding and training, the Lone Ranger saddles up Silver and with Tonto goes off in search of and then vanquishes Butch Cavendish.

In addition to radio, the Lone Ranger also saddled up Silver for the silver screen. A fifteen-part movie serial, *The Lone Ranger*, heralded Silver's screen debut in 1938. Silver had second billing, ahead of Tonto. In 1956, Clayton Moore—the most famous of the actors to play the masked man—and Jay Silverheels mounted their respective steeds for *The Lone Ranger*. Out of 109 feature films released that year, *The Lone Ranger* ranked 65th and had a domestic gross of $1.5 million. A second feature with the same leads followed in 1958, *The Lone Ranger and The Lost City of Gold*. In 1981, Klinton Spilsbury donned the black mask and rode Silver in *The Legend of the Lone Ranger*. Several horses played Silver in the various films.

Clayton Moore and Jay Silverheels were selected to play the Lone Ranger and Tonto in *The Lone Ranger* television series (Moore left the series in 1952 but rejoined the cast in 1954). A stuntman before becoming an actor, Moore actually did the running leaps onto Silver.

Traveler was pure white, but he wasn't all white. Clayton Moore discovered a slightly-less-than-dime-size black spot in the horse's ear. He kept mum about the discovery and used the mark as a means of identifying his favorite horse.

According to Whitey Hughes, who used to exercise Traveler, the horse was the pride of the business at that time and a recognizable steed. "I'd take him for a three- or four-mile ride through Griffith Park, and people just stopped and looked at him. They just almost knew who he was." Although recognizable, Traveler was also high strung. "If he didn't like you, he'd reach out and nip you," Hughes said. "But he liked me, and he let me come into his stall. A lot of people he wouldn't let into the stall. Clayton Moore got along with him great. Traveler was full of fire, and he was ready for action, but he was very gentle."

Moore was amazed at the talent that Traveler displayed. The horse could grin, bow, nuzzle someone, untie a rope, and dance.

The cue for Silver's most famous trick—rearing up on his hind legs—was through the horse's reins. But Moore had second thoughts about the placement of this cue. Moore and Silver made personal appearances around the country to promote the television series. Because children flocked to these appearances, Moore was concerned that a child grabbing the reins would unknowingly cue Silver to rear, creating a dangerous situation. Moore suggested—and the trainer approved—placing this cue on the horse's right shoulder instead.

Notable Tidbits

The horse that played Silver in *The Legend of the Lone Ranger* (1981), starring Klinton Spilsbury and Michael Horse, was a seven-year-old stallion owned by country singer Judy Lynn. Nearly 150 horses were used in the film's production.

TOTO

Real Name: Terry

Breed: Cairn terrier

Star Qualities: "I-Vant-To-Be-Alone" shyness. Before becoming a movie star, Terry was so shy that the poor pooch was more comfortable hiding underneath a bed rather than interacting with people.

Special Tricks: Escaping from baskets, jumping through open windows, grabbing a wiener from a roasting fork, leaping from a closing drawbridge, jumping out of a hot air balloon, following the Yellow Brick Road.

Most Famous Role: Toto in *The Wizard of Oz* (MGM, 1939)

Plot

Dorothy, a young Kansas girl, and her faithful dog Toto travel "Over the Rainbow" to a colorful land of curious people, including a Scarecrow, a Tin Woodman, a Cowardly Lion, and the Wicked Witch of the West. Through many strange adventures, Dorothy realizes that "there's no place like home," and with the power of ruby slippers and with the assistance of the Wizard of Oz, she returns to her Uncle Henry and Auntie Em.

Cast

Judy Garland	Dorothy
Frank Morgan	Professor Marvel/The Wizard of Oz
Ray Bolger	Hunk/the Scarecrow
Bert Lahr	Zeke/the Cowardly Lion
Jack Haley	Hickory/the Tin Woodman
Billie Burke	Glinda
Margaret Hamilton	Miss Gulch/Wicked Witch of the West
Charley Grapewin	Uncle Henry
Clara Blandick	Auntie Em
The Singer Midgets	The Munchkins
Terry	Toto

Adventures Behind the Scenes

The principal human roles in *The Wizard of Oz* were easy to cast compared to the ten-month long search made for the dog to play Toto. The staff in the property department at Metro-Goldwyn-Mayer were given a copy of author L. Frank Baum's book, *The Wonderful Wizard of Oz*, and were instructed to find a dog that resembled the book's illustrations of Toto. The property department puzzled over that assignment long and hard because no one recognized the breed of dog in the drawings done by illustrator W. W. Denslow.

The property department staff made copies of Denslow's drawings and circulated them to animal trainers across the United States and around the world, hoping that someone could identify the type of dog the artist had portrayed. Some thought the dog was a Scottie, so the staff put out a casting call for Scotties. Producer Mervyn LeRoy was unimpressed with every dog that was paraded past him. On September 1, 1938, *Daily Variety* columnist Alta Durant wrote that the producer was continuing to look for "a Scottie, a well-educated one, a dog intelligent enough to follow Judy Garland through several sequences of *The Wizard of Oz*," The columnist noted that by this time LeRoy had seen "every other known brand of canine with really remarkable IQs . . . but thus far no Scottie with sufficient education."

Toward the end of September 1938, dog trainer Carl Spitz happened upon a copy of

(*Archive Photos*)

W.W. Denslow's original illustration of Toto—Scottie or cairn terrier?

Denslow's drawings. He was certain that the dog was a cairn terrier, and he had just the pooch for the part, a cairn terrier named Terry. Spitz brought Terry to the studio and couldn't believe the reception the animal received. "The producer was there, the writer was there. Everyone," Spitz remembered. "And someone right away hollered, 'That's the dog we want.'"

Unfortunately, Spitz was unaware of the studio's desperation to cast a dog to play Toto. So Spitz agreed to a salary of $125 a week for Terry, making the terrier the lowest paid of the ten major actors. Judy Garland received the next lowest weekly salary—$500 — while Jack Haley and Ray Bolger received the highest weekly salaries— $3,000 each. "I didn't know how badly they needed the dog," Spitz said. "I could have gotten $500 a week."

Richard Thorpe, the original director of *The Wizard of Oz*, spent the first two weeks of filming shooting scenes in the Witch's Castle, including shots of Toto escaping from and returning to the castle to help rescue Dorothy. During the filming, Spitz positioned himself out of camera range and used hand signals to direct his dog. The director was thrilled at how well trained Terry was. According to Spitz, Thorpe "loved the little dog so much that the dog was finally the star—not Judy Garland." Producer Mervyn LeRoy was dissatisfied with the rushes, fired Thorpe, and threw out all the film that had been shot. Spitz said: "I was disgusted. So when they changed directors, I gave the dog over to another trainer to work. He worked three or four weeks and got suddenly very ill because the picture was so strenuous. And then I took over again."

Terry had a stand-in dog for rehearsals. For extended color and lighting tests, the "stand-in" was a small stuffed animal. Terry did all of the close-up work.

Terry had a difficult time on the set with the giant wind machines. The machines whipped up winds that knocked over the diminutive dog time after time. Terry soon learned to duck behind Garland, Bolger, Haley, or Lahr whenever the machines were in use.

In early December 1938, the film's third director, Victor Fleming, directed a scene at the Witch's Castle when the Witch's guards chase Toto. Unfortunately, during the scene, one of the guards accidentally stepped on Terry, spraining the dog's foot. Terry was out of commission for several weeks, causing Carl Spitz to look for a double. "I looked everywhere," Spitz said. "Finally, I raced up to San Francisco and found one. I took $350 of my money to buy the dog. Later, I found that a quarter of a mile down from my place on Riverside Drive was identically the dog like Toto, better than the $350 dog I had bought."

Memorable Movie Moment

Dorothy, the Scarecrow, the Tin Woodman, and the Cowardly Lion return to the palace of The Wizard, bearing the broomstick of the "liquidated" Wicked Witch of the West. Dorothy presents the broomstick and asks The Wizard to keep his promise about giving the Scarecrow some brains, the Tin Woodman a heart, the Cowardly Lion some courage, and sending Dorothy back home. The Wizard tells them that he has to give the matter some thought and orders them to come back the next day.

"Tomorrow?" Dorothy cries. "Oh, but I want to go home now."

As The Wizard angrily orders them away again, Toto scoots from Dorothy to a curtained area off to the side, and the curious canine disappears behind the curtain.

"If you were really great and powerful, you'd keep your promises," Dorothy scolds.

"Do you presume to criticize the great Oz?"

With teeth firmly on the bottom edge of the curtain, Toto pulls the curtain to reveal The Wizard to Dorothy and her friends.

She confronts The Wizard, and he admits that he is a humbug. The great and powerful Oz stands before Dorothy and her friends, embarrassed to have been exposed by clever little canine, Toto.

Notable Tidbits

Carl Spitz took up dog training as a hobby in his native Germany. He trained dogs for the deaf using hand signals. When Spitz emigrated to the United States in 1926 and settled in California, he became an animal trainer in the silent movie industry. In silent films, trainers shouted commands at their animals. He realized that the advent of talking films would require a different kind of training for animals, and Spitz was the first trainer to train his animals, including Terry, to respond to silent commands.

Carl Spitz acquired Terry four years before *The Wizard of Oz* was made. A breeder had sold Terry to an elderly couple living in Pasadena, but the dog was so shy that it hid under a bed for three weeks. The couple contacted the breeder, demanding that she return their money. The breeder got in touch with Spitz and asked him to train Terry. He agreed and worked with the terrier for seven weeks. After Terry was trained, the breeder returned, but she didn't have the money to pay Spitz. She offered to give him a run-down car instead, but he refused. She never returned to claim Terry, so Spitz added the dog to the others at his kennel.

Initially, Spitz had no intention of using Terry for film work. However, one day Metro-Goldwyn-Mayer director Clarence Brown spied Terry at Spitz's kennel and asked Spitz to use her in a film. The dog trainer refused the offer, insisting that Terry was too shy to work. But Brown persisted and told Spitz that if the trainer wouldn't work with the dog in the film that he would work the dog himself. "I told him he would have to live with the dog for two months before the dog would work for him," Spitz said. "I was wrong. He worked her through the whole picture, and I was amazed at how the dog progressed. And so then she was a picture dog." From that humble beginning, Terry went on to achieve fame in *The Wizard of Oz*.

After *The Wizard of Oz*, Terry was reunited with Margaret Hamilton (the Wicked Witch of the West) in *Twin Beds* (United Artists, 1942).

TRIGGER

Real Name: Golden Cloud (originally)

Breed: Golden palomino

Star Qualities: Intelligence. According to his trainer Glenn Randall, "he was a very exceptional horse. The title he had of 'The Smartest Horse in the Movies' absolutely fit."

Special Tricks: Trigger could perform 60 tricks and needed only a word cue to execute 40 of them. He could walk 150 feet on his hind legs and drink from a milk bottle. Trigger was also a mathematical whiz—he could count to 20 and do simple addition and subtraction. Among his most difficult tricks was holding a pencil in his mouth and signing his name with an "X."

Most Famous Role: Trigger in more than 80 Roy Rogers films and in more than 100 episodes of the television series *The Roy Rogers Show* (1951–1957) with Roy Rogers and Dale Evans.

Story Line

Set in Mineral City, *The Roy Rogers Show* was a modern-day Western that featured Roy as the owner of the Double R Bar Ranch, Pat Brady as his sidekick with a cantankerous old army jeep he called Nellybelle, and Dale as the proprietor of the Eureka Cafe. Episodes related their efforts to solve problems and right wrongs.

Cast

Roy Rogers	Roy Rogers
Dale Evans	Dale Evans
Pat Brady	Pat Brady
Trigger	Trigger
Buttermilk	Buttermilk
Bullet	Bullet

Adventures Behind the Scenes

Sired by a Thoroughbred race horse by a palomino dam, Golden Cloud belonged to

Roy Rogers, Trigger, and Bullet the Wonder Dog in *The Roy Rogers Show*. (*Movie Star News*)

Hudkins Rental Stable in Hollywood, a company that leased horses to movie studios. Roy Rogers was beginning his series of Western films at Republic Pictures and needed a horse, so the studio asked the various stables to show their best horses to Rogers. Among the half dozen horses brought for Rogers' consideration was Golden Cloud, a magnificent stallion that had had some film experience: He had been the horse that Olivia de Havilland as Maid Marian rode through Sherwood Forest in the 1938 film, *The Adventures of Robin Hood*, starring Errol Flynn. Rogers rode the first horse and then the second horse down the street and back. Then he tried Golden Cloud. "As I hit an easy lope, then a fast gallop, I could feel that this boy was an athlete with power to spare and fine balance that would set him in good stead for chases over rocky grades and down steep mountain slopes," Rogers said. Rogers didn't bother riding any of the other horses; he had found the mount that suited him.

Soon after the agreement was reached to lease Golden Cloud to Republic for Rogers's first film, *Under Western Stars*, the cowboy actor was on the set practicing his quick draw. Watching him were Smiley Burnette and others, and the conversation turned to Rogers's new horse and the fact that Golden Cloud could outrun any horse on the set. According to Rogers, Burnette said "As fast and as quick as the horse is, you ought to call him Trigger. You know, quick-on-the-trigger." Rogers thought that was a good name, and Golden Cloud was called Trigger from that day on.

Because Trigger was leased by the studio, he could not accompany Rogers on the publicity tour for the first film. At every city and town where Rogers stopped, folks were thrilled to see him but wanted to see Trigger, too. When Rogers returned from the tour, he visited the Hudkins Stable and struck a deal with Clyde Hudkins to buy Trigger. The asking price? Hudkins wanted $2,500. Although Rogers was making only $75 a week, he agreed to the deal. "I paid him off on time, just like you would a bedroom set," Rogers said. "It seemed like a lot of money back then, but I can tell you for sure and certain that it was the best $2,500 I ever spent."

Throughout his career, Trigger could always rely on four or five look-alike palomino horses to act as stand-ins for long-distance shots. However, Trigger always acted in the close-up shots, including chases over mountains, down steep grades, and through rocks. According to Rogers, "He was tough. If you gave him a little breather after each one, he could just go all day. I'm the only cowboy in the business, I think, that started and made all my pictures with one horse."

Trainer Glenn Randall worked with Roy Rogers and Trigger for twenty-four years. Trigger was stabled at Randall's spread in North Hollywood so that horse and trainer could work together every day. "He was exceptionally good at mouth work," Randall said. Trigger was an expert at untying a rope, retrieving objects, pulling a pistol out of a holster, and removing a rope from a saddle. He could even play jump rope. With Trigger holding one end of a rope and Randall holding the other end, the pair swung the rope, allowing Rogers to jump the rope.

Notable Tidbits

As a publicity stunt for their first appearance at Madison Square Garden, Rogers brought Trigger into the Hotel Dixie on Forty-Third Street in Times Square, where the cowboy star was staying. Wearing special rubber-soled, leather shoes, Trigger walked into the lobby and up to the front desk. There he found a pencil, grabbed it with his lips, and used the pencil to sign the guest register with his "X." Then Trigger and Rogers met with the media for a press conference. Some observers might have worried about Trigger's soiling the carpeting unexpectedly, but that was not a problem. Trigger was completely housebroken and knew when to go outside to take care of another kind of business.

Trigger had an understudy called Trigger, Jr., who was used for personal appearances. According to Rogers, "He wasn't worth a nickel as a cowboy horse, but he could do a beautiful dance routine." Trigger, Jr., could perform a Spanish march, a Spanish trot, and the hoochie-coochie.

Trigger rallied the support of the homefront during World War II. When sugar was rationed, Rogers and Trigger made a personal appearance in Washington, D.C., with Trigger wearing a sign stating: "I'm giving up sugar for the duration. That's horse sense."

In 1943, Franklin D. Roosevelt invited Rogers and a number of other Hollywood

Trigger got top billing with Roy Rogers in his films.

celebrities to the White House for a March of Dimes Ball. "Mrs. Roosevelt came along, tapped me on the shoulder, and invited me back to the kitchen," Rogers said. "She asked the chef to make us some hamburgers, which we ate with our hands, and we gabbed all night about one of my favorite subjects and hers: Trigger!"

"Because Trigger was smart, he figured out some pretty darn good kinds of mischief," Rogers said. Trigger's favorite bit of mischief involved creeping up behind Rogers while he was singing a religious song during personal appearances. Then, while the audience thought that the horse was giving Rogers a loving nuzzle, Trigger actually grabbed a mouthful of satin shirt and skin from Rogers' back or shoulder. "He bit and held on, hard enough to leave a big bruise afterwards," Rogers said. "It hurt like heck, and that ol' horse was smart enough to know that I couldn't scream with pain in the middle of 'Peace in the Valley' and I sure as shootin' couldn't turn around and whale him."

On movie sets, Trigger engaged in another type of mischief. When a horse was not needed for a scene, the trainer sometimes hobbled it. Similar to a pair of loose handcuffs, a hobble is placed around the horse's legs to keep the animal from wandering around. Hobbles were not enough to stop Trigger, who liked to be where the action was. He taught himself the hobble hop. Rogers said: "Even wearing hobbles, he developed a way of making tiny little jumps so no matter where we parked him, you could bet he'd show up where he wasn't supposed to be."

In 1946, Trigger had the tables turned on him and was himself the victim of mischief. Glenn Randall and Trigger were traveling to Hereford Heaven, Oklahoma, to shoot exterior scenes for *Home in Oklahoma*. Randall stopped at a small-town cafe, parked the open horse trailer, and went inside the restaurant for lunch. When he returned, he discovered that in his absence someone had hacked off a large portion of Trigger's flowing white tail, leaving only a straggly stump. When Randall and Trigger arrived on the set, the studio's hairdresser had to quickly fashion an artificial tail so that filming could be completed. "His tail took almost two full years to grow back, and from then on Trigger rarely made appearances without a backup tail or two just in case," Rogers said.

On April 21, 1949, Rogers and Trigger put their foot and hoof prints into wet cement at Grauman's Chinese Theater. It represented the height of their success.

In 1953, Trigger won a PATSY Award for his work in the 1952 film *Son of Paleface*, starring Bob Hope, Jane Russell, and Roy Rogers. In 1958 the American Humane Association granted Trigger the Craven Award, a special honor given to animals specializing in stunt work.

When Trigger died in 1965, Rogers had the horse's remains mounted and placed on display at the Roy Rogers and Dale Evans Museum in Victorville, California. Trigger stands reared up on his hind legs with a silver saddle on his back and bit and bridle in place. "He looks beautiful. I'm so happy I did it," Rogers said. "He appeared in all my pictures and countless personal appearances. It would have been a crime to bury him."

VERA

Real Name: Tai

Species: Asian elephant

Star Qualities: Consummate actress. According to *Larger Than Life* co-star Bill Murray, "Tai is undoubtedly the biggest star I've ever worked with. She's the smartest elephant in the world and very funny, and—even without any lines—she's as savage an upstager as I've ever known."

Special Tricks: Tai can respond to more than 50 voice commands and behaviors. Despite her gargantuan size—she weighs in at nearly 8,000 pounds—she can turn on a dime, a valuable asset when working within the often close confines of a movie set.

Most Famous Role: Vera in *Larger Than Life* (United Artists, 1996)

Plot

A motivational speaker whose philosophy for weathering the rough patches of life is to "get over it," Jack Corcoran discovers that his father did not die a hero many years before as Jack had been raised to believe. In truth, his father—a circus clown—has just now died, leav-

Vera shows Bill Murray a trick. (© *United Artists, photograph by Louis Goldman*)

ing Jack a trained circus elephant named Vera and a trunkful of debts. Determined to unload the pachyderm to pay off his father's bills, Jack embarks on a hilarious cross-country odyssey with the elephant, hoping to reach Los Angeles within five days to close a deal.

Cast

Bill Murray	Jack Corcoran
Janeane Garofalo	Mo Newman
Matthew McConaughey	Tip Tucker
Keith David	Hurst
Pat Hingle	Vernon
Jeremy Piven	Walter
Lois Smith	Luluna
Anita Gillette	Mom
Maureen Mueller	Celeste
Linda Fiorentino	Terry Bonura
Tai	Vera

Adventures Behind the Scenes

Producer Richard B. Lewis had some initial reservations about casting the role of Vera

Vera is a little reluctant about boarding a train for Kansas City.
(© *United Artists, photograph by Louis Goldman*)

in *Larger Than Life.* "When we started this process, we wondered how we were ever going to find an elephant to do all the things that were incorporated into the script," Lewis said. Lewis and his fellow producers John Watson and Pen Densham had heard good things about Tai from other filmmakers. "For the sake of my own sanity, I needed to check out Tai for myself," Watson said. He headed to Tai's home, the Have Trunk Will Travel elephant ranch owned by Gary and Kari Johnson in Perris, California.

At the ranch, Watson walked around Tai's enormous legs, and Tai took the producer for a ride around the acreage. Watson felt more comfortable about her, but he had one serious concern. "Elephants have keen survival instincts," he said. "They won't put themselves in danger; they won't stand in deep waters, or strain their trunks; when their trunks are tired, they simply let go. We talked about using prosthetic devices for certain situations, but once we started working with Tai, it quickly became apparent to us that it was unnecessary. She is truly an amazing elephant."

In the film, Jack and Vera begin their travels in the eastern United States and wind their way to California through deserts and over mountains. Filming was accomplished at a variety of locations in Missouri, Colorado, Illinois, Utah, and northern and southern California. Tai and her stand-in, Kitty, were troupers and seemed to enjoy the various locales.

According to director Howard Franklin, "Tai is as intelligent and gentle as you could hope for." However, the mammoth Tai posed a major challenge for Franklin. "It's hard to get a two-shot that holds a man and an elephant without getting back a ways or to find an angle where the actor, the background, and the world at large aren't blocked. And when you're scouting locations, a measuring tape is coming out all the time. Can she pass through here? Will she be able to walk up this alley? Will she be able to negotiate this corner?"

Possessed of unusual patience and a sweet personality, Tai was clearly an experienced actress on the set. Amidst the set's routine hullabaloo, she made her way delicately and masterfully over power cables, in between lighting equipment, and around myriad props. The crew and Tai's trainers took great care to ensure the elephant's safety and comfort.

Bill Murray, who played Jack Corcoran, seemed a bit envious of the star treatment accorded to Tai. At the time he said, "The elephant has better hours, gets to eat a lot more, and has better working conditions all the way around. Maybe I've just got to put on six or seven thousand pounds before I get that kind of respect." Murray had a long way to go in beefing up to match Tai. She ate 200 pounds of food a day.

Utah provided the perfect setting for the Native American village where Vera proves herself a heroine. "That scene," according to producer Richard B. Lewis, "is a turning point in the film for Jack. Jack's objective until that point had been to rid himself of Vera. But when he stumbles onto a village in distress and Vera acts to help these people, Jack begins to understand that this mere animal is capable of a selfless act beyond anything Jack was willing or able to perform."

Memorable Movie Moment

Jack Corcoran dupes a wildly paranoid trucker named Tip Tucker into carting him and Vera cross country. But Jack soon regrets the success of his con job when Tucker inundates him with a nonstop diatribe that is as incoherent as it is outrageous.

Notable Tidbits

Tai's previous acting credits included the central role in the comedy *Operation Dumbo Drop* (1995). She was also in *Rudyard Kipling's The Jungle Book* (1994) and *Made in America* (1993). She has had a successful commercial career as well and has made live appearances in numerous special events and parades.

Real Name: Keiko
Species: Orca (killer whale)
Star Qualities: Intelligence. Keiko adopted new behaviors quickly.
Special Tricks: Keiko can do breaches (leaps out of the water), bows, barrel rolls, high-speed swims, and games such as find-the-fish and chase-the-trainer.
Most Famous Role: Willy in *Free Willy* (Warner Bros., 1993)

Plot

A street-tough, twelve-year-old boy, ordered to remove painted graffiti from the walls of an aquarium, is at first frightened and then fascinated by the aquarium's killer whale. The boy befriends and trains the orca then helps him gain his freedom from the unscrupulous adventure park owners.

Cast

Jason James Richter . . . . Jesse
Lori Petty . . . . Rae Lindley
Jayne Atkinson . . . . Annie Greenwood
August Schellenberg . . . . Randolph Johnson
Michael Madsen. . . . . Glen Greenwood
Michael Ironside. . . . . Dial
Richard Riehle . . . . Wade
Mykelti Williamson. . . . . Dwight Mercer
Keiko . . . . Willy

Adventures Behind the Scenes

No behind-the-scenes story of a Hollywood animal actor is as dramatic as that of Keiko, the killer whale. Born into a close-knit society of orcas, Keiko was barely two years old when, in 1979, he and his family followed a boat hauling a huge catch of the whales' favorite food—herring—in the North Atlantic near Iceland. In a feeding frenzy, Keiko became ensnared by the boat's net. Generally, herring boat operators release trapped whales before they are harmed or before nets are damaged. But whale traders had promised the boat's captain thousands of dollars for the capture of a baby orca. Keiko was captured and transported to Saedyrasafnid, an Icelandic aquarium.

In 1982, Keiko was sold to Marineland in Ontario, Canada, where he joined six other whales being trained for eventual sale to amusement parks. As the youngest of the six, Keiko endured harassment from the other whales. He became timid, withdrawn, and as a result was less marketable. In 1985 Keiko was sold for $350,000 to Reino Aventura, an amusement park in Mexico City. He quickly became their star attraction, and within seven years he grew bigger in size and in celebrity status.

Around the time that Keiko was sold to Reino Aventura, a script about a boy who liberates a killer whale arrived at Warner Bros. The production team liked the basic story but thought that the script needed punching up. The script went through two rewrites, but the studio was uncertain about the box-office draw of a whale. Viewing footage of Pacific Ocean orcas convinced studio executives to approve a $20 million budget for the film in 1991.

Casting Willy, the animal star of the film, involved finding a young, solo whale in a plain tank. Keiko in Reino Aventura fit the bill. Location filming took place at the Mexican amusement park in 1992. However, the production team needed to supplement the footage. Whale effects supervisor Walt Conti and his robotics technicians worked their movie magic by creating several small versions of Willy as well as a full-scale, 22-foot, rubber-coated whale that was an exact animatronic (live-action robot) double of Keiko. The combination of live Keiko action, animatronics, and computer-generated imagery created stunning sequences such as Willy's saving Jesse from drowning and Willy's soar to freedom over the sea wall.

To call attention to the plight of whales, the filmmakers included a toll-free number at the conclusion of *Free Willy* for anyone who wanted more information about aiding the world's whales. According to producer Lauren Schuler-Donner, when the film was previewed

Keiko touched a lot of people in *Free Willy*. (*Courtesy of Oregon Coast Aquarium, photograph by Larry Cantrall*)

in November 1992, "it tested through the roof. Even the focus groups wanted to donate to the whale foundation."

Free Willy not only enjoyed rave reviews but a whale of a box-office opening—$7.8 million. The film that had started out as a "sleeper" became a blockbuster and soon had people all over the world wide awake and wanting to help whales such as Keiko. Within several months of the film's debut, more than 300,000 calls were made to the toll-free telephone number shown at the end of the film, especially after a *Life* magazine article revealed the inadequacy of Keiko's facility at Reino Aventura and the chronic health problems from which he suffered.

Memorable Movie Moment

Through the intense efforts of Jesse, Rae, Randolph, and the Greenwoods, Willy bursts through the water and soars in slow motion over a sea wall to the freedom of the ocean beyond.

Notable Tidbits

With Reino Aventura's approval and cooperation, Warner Bros. and the producers of *Free Willy* contacted whale protection activist David Phillips, of the Earth Island Institute in San Francisco, with the goal of formulating a rescue plan for Keiko. "This had never been done before. There'd never been a tie-in between a major Hollywood film and a conservation organization working to save wildlife," Phillips said.

Now Keiko has a comfortable home in the 2-million-gallon, natural sea water pool at Oregon Coast Aquarium in Newport. (*Courtesy of Oregon Coast Aquarium, photograph by Larry Cantrall*)

In November 1994, the Free Willy-Keiko Foundation was formed with $4 million donated by Warner Bros., New Regency Productions, and the McCaw Foundation. The Free Willy-Keiko Foundation's goal was Keiko's relocation and rehabilitation at a new facility and his eventual release back into the wild. Medical tests conducted on Keiko revealed a weakened immune system, an atrophied dorsal fin, and a skin rash caused by papillomavirus with lesions the size of turkey platters.

Three months later, Reino Aventura and the Free Willy-Keiko Foundation announced that Reino Aventura would donate Keiko to the Free Willy-Keiko Foundation and that construction would start immediately on a new $7.3 million rehabilitation facility for Keiko, to be built at the Oregon Coast Aquarium. The announcement brought a $1 million commitment from the Humane Society of the United States and launched a series of fundraising efforts across the country and around the world. The efforts by school children alone raised nearly $100,000 for Keiko's new home.

In mid-December 1995, more than 20,000 people filed past Keiko's small pool at Reino Aventura, saying good-bye to their special friend. Keiko's last public performance was a sold-out spectacular.

On January 7, 1996, after months of detailed planning, Keiko was maneuvered into a giant custom-made sling, hoisted by crane into a cargo container, and loaded aboard a C-130 cargo plane donated by United Parcel Service. Three thousand pounds of ice were added to the water in Keiko's container to keep the warm-blooded animal from overheating. Then

Keiko was flown from Mexico City to the Newport Municipal Airport, an event covered by a 350-member press corps representing more than 100 news organizations from around the world. After a twenty-hour international journey beset with mechanical delays and threats of bad weather, Keiko arrived at his brand-new, 2 million-gallon, natural sea water pool at the Oregon Coast Aquarium in the tiny town of Newport.

Keiko's arrival made him front-page news, a television celebrity, and an overnight sensation. His exploits were covered by many national newspapers and magazines, including *Life* and *People*, and he was featured on the *Today* show.

Within six months of his arrival at his new home, Keiko gained more than 1,000 pounds and added a foot to his length. His skin virus had almost completely healed. According to his veterinarian, Dr. Lanny Cornell, the combination of cold, natural sea water, improved diet, and freedom from the stress of performing contributed to Keiko's better health.

To facilitate his eventual release into his native Icelandic waters, Keiko undergoes training in hunting behaviors so that he will gain the independence necessary for survival in the wild. Researchers also study his vocalizations so that his particular whale sounds can be compared to the dialects "spoken" by the orca families residing in the North Atlantic. Because each killer whale family shares a few specific sounds unique to that family, Keiko's vocalizations may help to reunite him eventually with his family of origin.

WISHBONE

Real Name: Soccer

Breed: Jack Russell terrier

Star Qualities: Photogenic. Soccer has a wide, flat head; slightly pointed muzzle; black nose and lips. His small, v-shaped ears fall forward, and he has almond-shaped, deep-set, dark brown eyes. His body is predominantly white with a combination of tan and brown markings.

Special Tricks: Soccer can do a back flip; sit up; retrieve a ball; jump on and off chairs, sofas, and beds; raise his front paw; dig; and crawl.

Most Famous Role: Wishbone in the television series *Wishbone* (public television, debuted in 1995)

Story Line

In each live-action episode, Wishbone's real-life adventures with the children and families of the fictional town of Oakdale trigger a series of daydreams in which the perky pooch imagines himself as a character in a story from classic literature. The modern-day scenes parallel the story lines from literature, emphasizing the timeless and universal themes explored in these tales and encouraging a love of reading.

Cast

Jordan Wall . . . . Joe Talbot
Adam Springfield . . . . David Barnes
Christie Abbott. . . . . Samantha Kepler
Mary Chris Wall. . . . . Ellen Talbot
Angee Hughes . . . . Wanda Gilmore
Soccer. . . . . Wishbone

Adventures Behind the Scenes

Animal trainer Jackie Martin Kaptan was seeking a dog with a special look—"a character-looking dog with a sock eye"—and put the word out to breeders. A breeder of Jack Russells telephoned Kaptan, indicating she had a new puppy that was close to the look she was seeking. The breeder sent Kaptan a photograph of the puppy, and Kaptan was impressed with his markings—a solid brown right ear, a white left ear mottled with tan, and a left eye shadowed in brown. She purchased the eight-week-old puppy, named him Soccer, and began training him when he was one year old. "I was really lucky that he turned out to be such a good working dog," Kaptan said.

Soccer competed against more than 100 other dogs in a California casting call for the top-dog role in *Wishbone*. Before breaking into the big time with his first major television series, Soccer appeared in television commercials for Chuck Wagon and Mighty Dog; posed for several print advertisements, including a photo shoot for Nike; and had bit parts in feature films and in television shows.

For each *Wishbone* episode, the crew created a completely new, classic-literature setting—from ancient Greece and the wilds of Africa to nineteenth-century London to America during the Civil War. The show is filmed and produced at Lyrick Studios near Dallas on a 50,000 square-foot sound stage and a 10-acre back lot created specifically for the program. Each setting includes vehicles, buildings, rooms, furniture, other set details, and costumes for the actors and Soccer.

Wishbone has a wardrobe of 120 costumes, including Sherlock Holmes, Cyrano de Bergerac, Rip Van Winkle, Dr. Frankenstein, Silas Marner, and Hercules. His trainer's favorite costume is Robin Hood. "He looks buff," Kaptan said, "like Bruce Willis."

The costumes are nothing new to Soccer. Jack Russells typically get cold easily, so Soccer has worn sweaters and coats since he was a puppy. "He's never had the hats, and that was a little bit different for him," Kaptan said. "We had to do some training to get him used to the hats so he wouldn't shake them and want to pull them off his head."

In the episode "Rushin' to the Bone," Wishbone teased his audience with an inside joke about his costumes. In that episode, Wishbone has the chance to be the new Mr. MacPooch, national television representative for Mr. MacPooch Dog Biscuits. On the day Wishbone and friends arrive on the set, the director welcomes his star, and the crew bursts into applause.

"*Hmmm. I'd always heard that every dog has his day,*" Wishbone thinks.

"Chop, chop, now everyone. Now we must start rehearsal immediately. Now Renada will be taking care of his makeup," the director begins.

Wishbone as Hercules in "Hercules Unleashed." (© *Big Feats! Entertainment. Reprinted with permission.*)

"*Makeup!?!*" Wishbone thinks.

"And Stefano will be handling the costume."

"*Costume!?! What kind of a dog wears a costume!?!*"

Wishbone is displeased with wearing a Scottish kilt for the commercial in the modern-day sequence, but seems more comfortable in the fantasy sequence wearing Russian garb as Ossip, servant to Hlestakov, from *Inspector General* by Gogol.

A repertory company consisting of twenty-four classically trained actors from the Dallas area perform various roles from classic literary scenes in each episode of *Wishbone*. Classically trained in dog obedience and other amazing behaviors, Soccer performs about eighty percent of the on-screen work. Soccer works with a double named Bear and a stunt dog named Shiner.

Soccer portrays Wishbone as an articulate, clever, and funny character whose every thought is heard by the audience. The voice of Wishbone is provided by Larry Brantley, a former stand-up comedian and radio spokesperson. Soccer and Larry do not work together. Instead, Larry does his voice-overs off the set in a production booth the cast and crew call the "dog house."

Soccer finds his acting motivation in pieces of cooked beef or chicken, praise from his trainer, and toys. Although Soccer has a squeaky toy of which he is particularly fond, according to Jackie Kaptan, "I don't think there's been a toy invented that he wouldn't play with." Soccer also enjoys working with young actors. "Soccer likes kids," Kaptan said. "So working on the set for him is just one big party." Kaptan encourages the young actors to play with Soccer because the bonding that occurs and the level of comfort achieved helps the dog's performance.

Soccer works a 12-hour day on the set. Between scenes, he relaxes by playing or catching 40 winks in his quiet room.

Notable Tidbits

In 1996, Soccer, his trainer, and other members of the *Wishbone* cast participated in a multicity national promotional tour, making appearances in schools and shopping malls. "Kids just love him," Kaptan said. Kaptan believes that Wishbone's appearances are for a good cause—introducing young readers to some of the greatest masterpieces of world literature through "a little dog with a big imagination™."

Soccer probably did his signature flip when he learned that *Wishbone* was named by *USA Today* as "the best new kids' show." The series was awarded a Daytime Emmy in May 1996 and was nominated for the coveted Prix Jeunesse International for outstanding children's programming. Other honors include the Television Critics Association Award, Parents' Choice National Television Approval, a KIDS FIRST! endorsement, an American Association of School Administrators endorsement, a Seal of Approval for Quality Television from The Family Channel, and an award as Television Program of the Year from the Texas Film and Television Association.

Real Name: Cody

Breed: Malamute

Star Qualities: Aloofness. "Cody is supposed to be Sully's wolf," said Dennis Grisco of Grisco's Animals. "He's not supposed to be a Lassie. Wherever you see Sully, you'll see Wolf in the background. To maintain Cody's aloofness, Grisco keeps interactions between the dog and other cast members to a minimum.

Special Tricks: Dramatic mock attack. Cody can leap from a ramp, travel ten feet in the air, and land on someone. "He loves to do it," Grisco said. "I don't particularly love to do it because of his 85 pounds coming at me." Grisco often doubles for the actor playing the victim of Cody's mock attack.

Most Famous Role: Wolf in the television series *Dr. Quinn, Medicine Woman* (CBS, debuted in 1993)

Story Line

A Bostonian physician continually dismissed solely because of her gender travels to the Colorado Territory to set up a practice in Colorado Springs. The townsfolk resist the idea of a lady doctor, but with the help of three foster children and the local mountain man, the medicine woman is begrudgingly accepted as the town doctor. Episodes relate the trials, tragedies, and triumphs of forging a life and professional career on the frontier.

Cast

Jane Seymour	Dr. Michaela Quinn
Joe Lando	Byron Sully
Chad Allen	Matthew Cooper
Jessica Bowman	Colleen Cooper
Shawn Toovey	Brian Cooper
Barbara Babcock	Dorothy Jennings
Orson Bean	Loren Bray
Cody	Wolf

Adventures Behind the Scenes

Trainer Dennis Grisco obtained Cody when the dog was two years old. The family that owned him was going through a divorce and a move and could no longer keep the animal. Renowned animal trainer Karl Lewis Miller (*Beethoven, Babe*) agreed to take the dog and find him a good home. Miller offered the dog to Grisco, and he welcomed Cody to his kennel. But Grisco did not realize the dog's star potential until a job offer came along that Grisco thought would be perfect for the malamute and began training him.

According to Grisco, Cody is very intelligent. He learned basic dog obedience, and on cue he can snarl, retrieve, sit up, and dig. Most amazing is what he can do with his tail. "All malamutes have a curled tail, so he's been taught to hold his tail down like a wolf," Grisco said. This behavior worked to Cody's advantage and led to roles as either a wolf or a dog. In fact, on *Dr. Quinn, Medicine Woman*, Cody was originally cast as a wolf. However, more currently, the story line portrays him as a wolf hybrid.

Cody is such a gentle animal that Grisco uses a stand-in dog, Mika, for Cody's snarling scenes. According to Grisco, "Cody is a lover, and Mika is the devil." Cody's other *Dr. Quinn* stand-ins include Chaz, Indy, and King.

Cody's motivators include affection from his owner/trainer Grisco and the assistant

Joe Lando, Cody (Wolf), and Jane Seymour. (*Archive Photos/fotos international*)

trainers who work with him plus food rewards. His favorites are stew meat, hot dogs, broiled chicken, and commercial dog food. In shooting a scene involving Joe Lando and Cody, Grisco gives Lando a food treat, which the actor shows to the dog and then places in his pocket. The scene begins and progresses to the end, the director yells "Cut!," then Lando pulls the treat from his pocket and rewards the dog.

One of Cody's star qualities is the naturalness of his acting, according to Grisco. "Most dogs look up at the actor anticipating the food treat. Cody just walks along. He doesn't stare at the trainer or actor all the time. When he gets the treat, he gets it. If he doesn't, that's fine. He's been doing this so long, he just acts so naturally. I get more compliments and more questions asking how I trained his behavior to go with an actor and not to act as if he's doing it on cue," Grisco said.

Notable Tidbits

Cody's first feature film was *The Lost Boys* (1987) a movie about teenage vampires. For that film, Cody played a family's pet malamute. Set in Alaska, *On Deadly Ground* (1994) with Steven Seagal, featured Cody as a mean sled dog. He has appeared in commercials for automobiles, a regional telephone company, and dog food.

MISCELLANEOUS MENAGERIE

Barkley looking debonair in his eye patch. With Valeria Golino (left) and Dana Carvey. (*Archive Photos/fotos international*)

BARKLEY

Walking into Walls Can Open Doors

The brown, white, and black Jack Russell terrier named Barkley is nothing if not a trouper. He completed seven feature films in five years plus managed to squeeze in roles on the television series *Burke's Law* and *Full House*. But the perky pooch hit it big with his role as the klutzy terrier lacking depth perception in the 1994 comedy film, *Clean Slate*, starring Dana Carvey as a detective who begins each morning with no memory.

"*Clean Slate* was probably one of the hardest things I've ever done," says Barkley's owner and trainer Doree Sitterly, "because we had to train things that no one's ever had to train before."

Because the character wore an eye patch and viewed everything two feet to the left of its actual position, Barkley had to simulate missing the marks for his food bowl as well as his doggie door. Sitterly trained Barkley for wall crashing by showing him a spot on the wall next to the doggie door. She commanded him to touch the spot, and he headed to the wall and put his nose against the spot. Then a puppet was substituted for Barkley, and the puppet slammed into the wall.

According to Sitterly, Barkley perceived the eye patch as a sign that it was show time and that he would be rewarded for his work. And that perception turned into reality because audiences howled at Barkley's hilarious antics.

BEN

And *The Life and Times of Grizzly Adams*

The 1976 film *The Life and Times of Grizzly Adams* starred animal trainer/handler Dan Haggerty as "Grizzly" Adams and a female grizzly bear named Bozo as Adams's friend, Ben. The film was loosely based on the story of mountain man James Capen "Grizzly" Adams who was often accompanied on his excursions from the wilderness into San Francisco by two unleashed grizzly bears. Haggerty's rugged good looks won him the role, while Bozo, a 400-pound former circus performer, was selected because of her work in 1970's *King of the Grizzlies*.

The success of the film led to the television series, *The Life and Times of Grizzly Adams* (1977–1978), to which both Haggerty and Bozo contributed their talents. Filmed at Wasatch National Forest near Park City, Utah, and at Payson, Arizona, the episodes related the adventures of a gentle man falsely accused of a crime who finds refuge in the peace offered by the wilderness and animals.

Owned by Lloyd Beebe of the Olympic Game Farm in Sequim, Washington, Bozo was an extraordinary animal with an unusual affection for humans, especially co-star Haggerty. The pair often enjoyed chasing each other through meadows, tumbling to the ground when one caught the other. Rolled over on her back, Bozo even allowed Haggerty to scratch her belly. Bozo was so easy going on the series that she could wander the set unleashed. By contrast, her four doubles were not only leashed but had their movements controlled by charged electrical wires.

Cued to perform by the sound of a buzzer, Bozo was rewarded with sweet treats such as fruit or marshmallows. But she had a habit of wanting to perform a scene over and over again to earn a treat even though the director had the required, satisfactory shots. Because of her sweet tooth, she packed on more than 100 pounds during the production of the series.

THE PERFECT BLACK STALLION

Cass Olé

To turn Walter Farley's novel, *The Black Stallion*, into a film, director Carroll Ballard searched the world for the perfect horse for the part. He ended his quest in San Antonio, Texas, where he found a purebred Arabian named Cass Olé. Although he was a well-known show horse, Cass Olé had no experience as a motion picture actor, so Ballard hired well-known trainer Corky Randall to prepare the horse for the role. Randall worked with Cass Olé for 11 weeks and was surprised at how quickly and how much the horse learned.

Cass Olé undertook his work in the film with gusto, revealing to those on the set that he was a classic Hollywood ham. According to Randall, "Cass really liked to be in front of the camera. He naturally likes being around people; in that respect, he's more like a dog than a horse."

Although Cass Olé was clearly the lead horse, he had a number of doubles to help with the film's animal action. For example, in a beach scene featuring boy and stallion, the horse was one of Cass Olé's stand-ins, a gray quarter horse dyed black.

Cass Olé himself was no stranger to a dye job. In the film he appears perfectly black, but he actually had four white socks on his legs and a white star on his forehead. Those spots

Kelly Reno and Cass Olé. (*Archive Photos/United Artists*)

were tinted black to match his description in the book. Another addition was his wig. Extra hair was plaited into his mane to bring his physical appearance more in line with author Farley's vision of the horse.

The Black Stallion (1979), starring Kelly Reno, Mickey Rooney, and Teri Garr, tells the story of a boy's adventures with a magnificent black stallion from the horror of a ship wreck to the triumph of a racing championship win.

The film made Cass Olé a star. He was signed to a seven-year contract with Francis Ford Coppola's Zoetrope Studios, was insured for $250,000, and watched his stud fee double to $1,500.

BRUCE

The Cat Who Was Sweet on *Honey West*

The character Honey West was a 1965 rarity—a female private investigator—but she was even more unusual in her choice of house pets. Played by Anne Francis in the series *Honey West* (1965–1966), West had inherited her father's detective business along with a partner, Sam Bolt (played by John Ericson). The sexy sleuth was skilled at judo and karate, had an amazing arsenal of high-tech weapons, and carried a lipstick that contained a radio transmitter. And at the conclusion of a rough-and-tumble day spent outwitting the bad guys, West cuddled up with the love of her life—her pet ocelot named Bruce. A purr-fect way to end the day.

THREE DOGS! THREE BUCKS! WHAT A DEAL!

Buck 1:

The first St. Bernard to become a star was not Beethoven but Buck, a male pedigreed dog whose role in the 1934 version of *Call of the Wild* with Clark Gable and Loretta Young made him famous.

Buck was not the first animal actor considered for the role in *Call of the Wild*. The original script called for the role to be filled by a German shepherd. A German shepherd was cast, but the dog looked too small next to he-man King of Hollywood Clark Gable. Director William Wellman decided to use a St. Bernard instead, and Buck answered the casting call.

Clark Gable and Buck in *Call of the Wild* (1934). (*Movie Star News*)

Buck and Gable were off-screen buddies. Gable lived in Hollywood near the home Buck shared with his trainer Carl Spitz. (Spitz also owned and trained Terry, the dog that played Toto in *The Wizard of Oz*.) Gable knew Carl and his wife Alice and visited the Spitz home often. When Buck wasn't acting, he enjoyed the run of the house, including sleeping in the master bedroom. Despite his size, he was a gentle animal who loved children and was a frequent guest at kiddie birthday parties, where he pulled young ones around in a specially-constructed wagon.

Filmed on location on the snowy slopes of Mount Baker, Washington, *Call of the Wild* was a grueling experience for Buck, other cast members, and crew. They battled below-zero weather, frequent white-outs, and diminished food supplies. Buck showed great flexibility under these hardships. When his usual commercial dog food was not available, he ate table scraps. But sometimes even table scraps were in short supply. Food for the company ran out several times, and expeditions of hearty souls were dispatched to distant towns to procure fresh provisions.

One of Buck's special talents was his ability to howl on cue. In *Call of the Wild*, Buck's character responds to the call of a she-wolf in the night, and he leaves to seek his mate. Carl Spitz used a small chain tucked in his pocket to cue Buck. When Buck was required to perform a trick or stunt, Spitz rattled the chain.

After *Call of the Wild* completed filming, the studio was so impressed with Buck's talents that he was signed to a long-term contract. His other films included *Melody Trail* (1935), *The Country Beyond* (1936), *Robinson Crusoe on Mystery Island* (1936), *Trigger*

Trio (1937), *Hold That Kiss* (1938), and *Call of the Yukon* (1938).

Unfortunately, Buck had a sad and mysterious end. In 1941, he unexpectedly became ill and suddenly died. An autopsy showed that he had been poisoned, although no one was ever charged with the crime. Buck's descendants stepped into his cinematic shoes, completing several of *The Road* films with Bing Crosby, Bob Hope, and Dorothy Lamour. For a "dynamite" Buck performance, check out *The Road to Utopia* (1945).

Buck 2:

A grandson of *Call of the Wild*'s Buck, this Buck had the featured role of a brandy-guzzling, drunken St. Bernard ghost in the fantasy-situation comedy *Topper* (1953–1957).

When the series began, Buck was cast in the role of Neil, an alcoholic dog whose trademark was the small cask of brandy that he carried around his neck. The premise of the show was simple yet fantastic: Wealthy gad-abouts, George and Marian Kirby (played by Robert Sterling and Anne Jeffreys) celebrate their fifth wedding anniversary by taking a skiing trip to Switzerland. While on the slopes, Marian falls. George schusses over to see if she is injured, and rescue dog Neil arrives to save them both. Rather than offering the brandy to Marian, Neil downs it himself. Suddenly from above, snow rumbles and tumbles, and buries the trio. When they emerge from the avalanche, George, Marian, and Neil discover that they have been killed and are now ghosts. Not knowing what else to do, they return to the Kirbys' old home, now occupied by a stuffy banker, Cosmo Topper (played by Leo G. Carroll) and his wife Henrietta (played by Lee Patrick) and become Topper's live-in ghosts. Topper is the only person able to see, hear, and speak with them.

The hilarity of the show came from the wise-cracking, unseen ghosts' interactions with Topper and with the various people who came through his life. One episode involved Neil stealing Topper's briefcase containing important bank documents. In another episode, George and Marian decide to give Neil a bath in the backyard. Henrietta sees only water splashing all over, not the ghostly threesome, and quickly summons Topper to explain the strange phenomenon. Always creative in his off-the-cuff rationalizations, he tells Henrietta that the water is "our new sprinkling system." Topper then scolds Marian about Neil's backyard bath. "He's got fleas," she retorts. "Fleas don't live on dead dogs," Topper says. Marian answers: "They're dead fleas."

Buck rehearsed his scenes three or four times before the camera rolled, and it took a bit of doing for him to get used to wearing an ice bag on his head to simulate weekly hangovers. He didn't seem to mind wearing the brandy cask—it contained not alcohol but a liquid mixture made of beef marrow.

Buck 3:

This Buck is no relation to Buck #1 or Buck #2. Buck #3's real name was Michael, but he played Buck, the Bundy's family pet, for eight seasons on the series *Married, With Children* and his stage name became the character's name. Buck was always his own man, but his voice was provided by Cheech Marin.

Buck was a trained adult Briard, a French breed of large, strong dogs. From the series' 1987 debut on, Buck saw it all with the odd-ball Bundy clan. In a 1987 episode "Buck Can Do It," patriarch Al Bundy was pressured by irate neighbors to have Buck neutered: Buck's "carnal trespassing" had resulted in "stupid, ugly puppies." In an episode the following season called "Master the Possibilities," the family went on a spending spree with an unsolicited new credit card in Buck's name. In 1993, the episode "Change for a Buck" showed a neglected and fed-up Buck running away from home. Unfortunately, the Bundys didn't discover his absence for a week, and all that time Buck was at the pound with his time limit ticking away.

Of course, Buck had his share of Bundy family celebrations. In 1994's "Assault and Batteries," Kelly and Bud held a birthday party for Buck. The following year, in "Twenty-Five Years and What Have You Got?" Buck buried Peg's wedding anniversary present in the backyard.

Buck retired in 1995 when he was almost thirteen years old. His farewell episode was "Requiem for a Dead Briard." In that episode, the Bundys return home after Buck's funeral. Meanwhile, the pathetic pooch stands at the Pearly Gates, hoping that his sad life with the Bundys will earn his spirit a reassignment. Grief-stricken by Buck's death, Kelly is not comforted by new pets or even a seance to make contact with Buck. Buck gets his wish and does return to earthly life. He is reincarnated as a cocker spaniel puppy named Lucky who is anything but—the pup comes to live at the Bundy house.

That episode ended with a special message to Buck: "Dedicated to Buck the Dog who with this episode begins a well-earned retirement and hopefully a nice gig at stud. We'll miss you, Buddy, lift a leg. The Producers." The end credits were shown over a picture of Buck.

After his retirement, Buck did make it through the Pearly Gates. He passed away, but for fans he remains a happy memory in *Married, With Children* reruns.

BULLET

Roy Rogers' Faithful Dog

Bullet the Wonder Dog had his Hollywood debut in *Spoilers of the Plains*, the last feature film that Roy Rogers made for Republic Pictures in 1951. When "The King of the Cowboys" moved to television, Bullet trotted along with him. This German shepherd was an accomplished canine actor, performing an unusual range of dog stunts through the more than 100 episodes of *The Roy Rogers Show* (1951–1964).

"We sent to Germany at the beginning of our TV series and bought an attack dog to be used only for special action scenes where Bullet, who was the most gentle animal, would not work so well," Rogers said.

The first time the double was used, the scene involved bad-guy actor Freddie Graham jumping on his horse and getting ready to ride away as a leaping Bullet latches onto the calf of his leg. Graham was outfitted with leather leg padding up to his knee to protect him during the scene.

Everything was set. Trainer Earl Johnson turned loose the double dog who ran after

Graham. But the dog leaped too high, catching the actor in the thigh. Forgetting that the dog did not understand English, Johnson repeatedly shouted "Stop!" to no avail. The dog tenaciously held on while the actor screamed. "Achtung! Achtung!" stopped the attack. Graham was taken to the hospital for emergency treatment and a tetanus shot.

Bullet, who was too lovable to chew someone's leg off, left all such rough-and-tumble action to the double, who was subsequently taught commands in English. After *The Roy Rogers Show* ended, Bullet romped and played the rest of his days on the Rogers' ranch. After Bullet's death, Rogers had his faithful dog mounted and placed in the Roy Rogers and Dale Evans Museum in Victorville, California.

BUTTERMILK

Dale Evans' Horse

Although born in Texas, "The Queen of the West" Dale Evans was not an experienced horsewoman when she began making Westerns with "The King of the Cowboys" Roy Rogers. In fact, in 1944, during the making of their first movie together, *The Cowboy and the Senorita*, Rogers suggested that if she wanted to stay alive Evans should take riding lessons. "After some time I got to the point where I could sit a horse pretty well. I *had* to ride well by the time I got Buttermilk," Evans said.

Evans rode a palomino named Pal in films and during live shows. Because Pal looked like Trigger's twin on a small television screen, a new horse named Buttermilk was used for *The Roy Rogers Show*. A pearl-color quarter horse with black mane and tail, Buttermilk became associated with Dale Evans in the same way that Trigger had become associated with Roy Rogers. While Trigger was gentle and kind, Evans characterized Buttermilk as "feisty." Because he had been used for roping, he was a nimble animal and often turned on a dime without warning, dumping his rider in the process. "One time he dumped our horse trainer Glenn Randall just to prove he could do it," Evans said.

As Buttermilk grew accustomed to working in front of a camera, the buzzer that signaled that the camera was rolling was like a starter's pistol for the spirited horse—he was off and running. Evans remembered one scene during which Pat Brady, an excellent horseman, was required to gallop away on Buttermilk. Evans said: "After he got off, he came over to me and said, 'Shoo, girl, you gotta ride every minute you're on that horse.'"

After Buttermilk's death, Roy Rogers had Evans' favorite horse mounted and placed in the Roy Rogers and Dale Evans Museum in Victorville, California.

CHAUNCEY

The Mercury Cougar

When a 200-pound cougar leaps onto a platform near an automobile-company sign and snarls, people pay attention. That animal was Chauncey, a trained cougar who represented the Mercury division of the Ford Motor Company in its television commercials.

Chauncey contributed his distinctive snarl, but because of an arthritic condition, the athletic work was provided by his doubles, Harold and Herman. Chauncey pulled down a cool $2,000 per week for his work and drove away with a PATSY Award in 1969. Nice being recognized by the industry and also by your audience—at one point, Chauncey was ranked third (behind Coke's bottle and Ford's oval emblem) on the list of the most readily recognized advertising symbols.

"ME TARZAN, YOU CHEETAH"

Cheetah was the cutest chimpanzee in the African jungle, providing help to his friend Tarzan in times of trouble and comic relief between action scenes in films and on television. Through the decades, numerous chimps have played the lovable Cheetah, the brainchild of author Edgar Rice Burroughs. The trainers who worked with the chimpanzees pre-

ferred to replace the animals every few years because, despite their adorable appearance, adult chimpanzees tend to be unpredictable and dangerous.

The most well-known Tarzan, Johnny Weissmuller, let his Cheetah know who would be boss when he met the chimp, named Jiggs, for the first time in 1931. As Jiggs bared his teeth aggressively, Weissmuller pulled his hunting knife from its sheath and flashed its shiny blade close to Jiggs' face. The chimp's dark eyes registered understanding. To make a stronger statement, Weissmuller knocked Jiggs' head with the knife. Weissmuller replaced the knife then extended his hand as a good-will gesture. Jiggs glared in anger, then grinned, and then after a moment shook Weissmuller's hand. They were friends.

However, Weissmuller's co-star,

Cheetah, Johnny Sheffield, Johnny Weissmuller, and Maureen O'Sullivan hang out together. (*Movie Star News*)

Maureen O'Sullivan, was not as fortunate. During the filming of *Tarzan, the Ape Man* (1932), some of O'Sullivan's hair blew into Jiggs' eyes. Temporarily blinded, the chimp bit O'Sullivan and rampaged through the set.

When Mike Henry played the loin-clothed lord in *Tarzan and the Great River* (1967), his Cheetah was a volatile chimp named Dinky. As Henry recalled, "I was to run over to the chimp and pick him up. When I did, he lashed out at me and ripped my jaw open. It took twenty stitches to put my face back together." Subsequently, Henry developed a monkey-fever delirium which wracked him for seventy-two hours, and he required three weeks to recuperate.

Television's Tarzan, Ron Ely, worked well with his Cheetah, a chimpanzee actually named Cheetah. The NBC series ran from 1966 through 1968, and during that time Ely collected his share of Cheetah's bites and scratches because Ely performed his own stunts. The fearless Ely did not seem at all intimidated by the danger, but the program's producer was scared to death that his star would be injured—he insured Ely for three million dollars.

CIRCUS BOY

Animals Under the Big Top

The television adventure series *Circus Boy* (1956–1958) shared the behind-the-scenes stories of performers and roustabouts in a turn-of-the-century traveling circus. Episodes were presented through the eyes of twelve-year-old Corky (played by Micky Braddock), an orphaned boy who had been adopted by the owner of the circus, Big Tim Champion (played by Robert Lowery). Animals under the Big Top included Bimbo, a baby elephant, who was Corky's pet; Sultan the tiger; Nuba the lion; and Hasan the horse.

Micky Braddock turned into an animal of sorts a decade later. As an adult, he used his real last name—Dolenz—and joined David Jones, Peter Tork, and Michael Nesmith as one of The Monkees.

DON'T MONKEY AROUND WITH CLYDE

In the 1978 film *Every Which Way but Loose*, Philo Beddoe (played by Clint Eastwood) is a trucker who earns extra money by challenging the toughest man in each area of the country to a bare-knuckle brawl. One such bout nets him an orangutan named Clyde, and the ape becomes his friend and traveling companion. This Clyde was owned and trained by Bobby Berosini, famous for his troupe of orangutan comics. In fact, Eastwood was in the audience during a performance by the Berosini orangutans and, impressed by their act, Eastwood struck a deal to use one of the animals in his film.

For the 1980 sequel, *Any Which Way You Can*, Eastwood used C.J., an orangutan owned and trained by Ralph Helfer. At a hefty 275 pounds, with thick reddish-gold fur and small, beady eyes, C.J. hit it off right away with Eastwood. According to Helfer, "His handling of C.J. was second nature—off-the-cuff and mellow. They would clearly be pals for life!"

In the film, Clyde has a signature move—using a right-hand turn signal to knock the bad guys off their motorcycles. C.J. adapted this move for use in real life. According to Helfer, when he and C.J. drove down the freeway and people recognized the ape as Clyde, they yelled out his name. Always playing to his audience, C.J. gave them his famous signal.

"C.J.'s outstanding talent and personality made him famous throughout the industry," Helfer said. C.J. enjoyed appearing on television talk shows, in cameo appearances in television series, and in motion pictures. In 1981, C.J. appeared with Bo Derek in *Tarzan, the Ape Man*. According to Helfer, "He was to the animal world what Laurence Olivier was to the human." C.J.'s talents were recognized. He was the recipient of a PATSY Award in 1983.

(*Archive Photos/fotos international*)

COMET

The Adventures of Brisco County, Jr.

"There wasn't one all-purpose Comet. The real beauty of filming with animals is getting the right one for the right trick," according to Bruce Campbell, hunky star of Fox's short-lived series *The Adventures of Brisco County, Jr.*, (1993–1994).

This wacky Western/fantasy featured Campbell as a nineteenth-century Harvard-educated lawyer turned maverick, wise-cracking bounty hunter, Brisco County, Jr., and Comet, a wonder horse who could do just about anything. Comet's capabilities included rearing, nodding and nudging his head, chewing his lip, stomping his foot, and even pulling brown-eyed, handsome manhunter Brisco and rival bounty hunter Lord Bowler (played by Julius Carry) from a bed of quicksand. All this action required five equines to share the role of Comet.

Copper was Campbell's main horse whom the actor nicknamed "Leadbelly." "He was an older horse who would just sit there. You could shoot off guns, and people could run around, and the horse was very quiet and calm," Campbell said. "Copper wasn't in the best of shape when we started. In the course of the season, this horse that I used to have to spur to get going, I ended up having to hold him back because he had gotten into better and better shape because he was running every day. It was good to see." Campbell admitted that at

(© Fox Broadcasting Company, photograph by Doug Hyun)

first Copper didn't like him—Campbell didn't know how to ride when he started the series—but eventually the two actors cultivated a mutual respect.

Strip was a trick horse who performed the head nods and nudges, the lip chewing, and the foot stomping. His coloring—the white star on his nose and the socks on his feet—was reproduced on the other horses by the makeup department. "Trick horses are very alert," Campbell said. "They're always looking over their shoulders for when they're going to do their next trick. They're more high strung. Strip was an incredibly smart horse but high strung. So I only rode Strip if we had to do some combination gag." Strip may have been high strung, but he was not camera shy; in fact, Campbell characterized him as a ham.

Strip's claim to fame was his lip chewing—as if he were speaking à la Mr. Ed. Unlike Mr. Ed's owner, Wilbur Post, who could hear his horse (of course, of course), Brisco had to imagine what smart aleck comments Comet made during their conversations. So that he could have a sense of what the horse was saying, Campbell had the script person concoct phony lines of dialogue so that the actor could respond to Comet's bon mots. "It's great to be able to have a scene where you talk to the horse. It becomes a really cool element of your work," Campbell said.

Comet's mouth movements were orchestrated by trainer Gordon Spencer who cued Strip off camera by wiggling a stick or by using verbal commands. When Strip performed correctly, he was allowed to enjoy a handful of grain. "I had a separate grain pocket sewn into my jacket, so I could reward the horse whenever he did something right that we had practiced," Campbell said.

Ace was the horse used for rearing. According to Campbell, great, strong Ace went up on his hind legs with a leg cue. "I'd give him a heel in the chest, and he'd go up," Campbell said. Ace was also cued by two long-handled sticks raised off camera by trainer Gordon Spencer. "When a horse rears, the trick is that you counter the weight," Campbell said. "As the horse goes up, you go forward. But you have to put your face to one side or the other, otherwise you'll get the horse's head right in your face."

Boss was a stunt horse for the stunt man in the action scenes and long shots. "That horse was really outrageous; he was just like a Porsche. He was a fine-tuned, powerful animal that you didn't really want to put an actor on—just a seasoned stunt man," Campbell said.

The fifth horse was used as a stand-in. "We actually called him **Comet** so he would become familiar with the name," Campbell said. When one of the four horses was out of sorts or acted fidgety, Comet was brought in complete with a matching saddle to play the scene as a double horse.

Campbell enjoyed his adventures as Brisco County, Jr., especially working with the horses. "You learn the personalities of every horse," Campbell said. "They are totally, one-hundred-percent distinct." Do you think Comet told him to say that?

CuJo

One Big, Bad St. Bernard

Known as a master of simulated violence, Karl Lewis Miller was the animal action expert for *Cujo*, the 1983 film starring Dee Wallace and Danny Pintauro as a mother and son terrorized by a rabid St. Bernard. Miller acquired eighteen dogs for the film from breeders, free-to-a-good-home newspaper ads, and families who needed to place problem dogs. After training all of them, Miller selected only four dogs to play the role of Cujo. The principal character dog was a gentle St. Bernard named Daddy.

The dog's deteriorating physical condition was created by using a gelatin mix for drool; putting a medicinal preparation in his eyes to make them look yellow and mucousy; and covering his coat with a mixture of movie blood, petroleum jelly, and movie dirt called fuller's earth. Daddy looked his worst for one of the movie's most frightening scenes—when mother and son are trapped in their car with mad, menacing Cujo ferociously pounding at the windshield, trying to break through the glass to get inside to attack them.

"He was just trying to get to his furry-covered squeaky mouse on the inside. The dog was just trying to get in to play," Miller explained. "We trained him on a table in my backyard with a piece of Plexiglas that I could collapse. The dog knew that if he kept pawing at it and pushing at it, the glass would collapse and then he could have his squeaky toy. By the time we got to the car on the set, the dog was just conditioned to keep pounding on the glass. Of course, the glass couldn't give in for the movie, so we tricked him. We made him think that the mouse came right through the glass to him if he pestered the glass enough."

Miller was the double who did all the bite scenes with Daddy. For two attack scenes, Miller wore a wet suit under his clothing, to cushion the dog's mouth activity, and had protective towels on the target bite areas. "Because it's all fast action, the viewer doesn't see the bulkiness of the material that the dog is biting on," Miller said.

The one scene Miller couldn't double occurs when Cujo goes for mom Donna Trenton's throat. The double for that scene was Miller's assistant trainer with a fur hamster squeaky toy tied to her throat. "The dog was actually leaping up trying to get to the toy," Miller said.

Adapted from the Stephen King novel, this film terrified audiences who were unaware of the marvelous movie magic that transformed sweet, lovable Daddy into dangerous, deadly Cujo.

SPOTTED ALL OVER TOWN

101 Dalmatians

Perdita and Pongo discuss their perky pups. (*Walt Disney Co./Everett Collection, photograph by Steve Gorton*)

In 1996's live-action update of the 1961 animated Disney classic, *101 Dalmations*, the murderous, fur-fashion fancier Cruella De Vil (played by Glenn Close) is up to her old tricks again. Wanting a full-length coat of genuine Dalmatian fur, De Vil hires henchmen Horace (Mark Williams) and Jasper (Hugh Laurie) to kidnap the puppies of parents Pongo and Perdy. The dim-witted duo succeeds, but the puppies escape and after some hilarious escapades are finally reunited with their owners, Roger (Jeff Daniels) and Anita (Joely Richardson).

Where did all those puppies come from? The film's production team placed ads in newspapers in the British Isles, asking Dalmatian breeders to contact the studio if they had litters they would be willing to lease. Disney Pictures picked up the tab for travel, accommodations, and other costs for the breeders to accompany their litters to the studio. To house each litter, the studio bank-rolled the building of deluxe kennels, complete with variable heating, an exercise run, and round-the-clock vets.

"We had to be extremely careful, as puppies are delicate," said chief animal trainer Gary Gero. "With up to 100 living in the same building, working together, eating together, and playing together, there was a risk that if one pup had something, they could all get it." The various stages were disinfected, and anyone entering a puppy area had to walk through disinfectant footbaths.

The production team had to balance a complex filming schedule with the availability of puppy litters plus the meal times, play times, and sleeping patterns of the various pups. According to Gero, "one of the real problems was the rate at which a puppy grows. The longest any puppy was with us was four weeks, but most of them stayed no longer than a week, especially those doing close-up work, where you really noticed their size. Puppies over twelve weeks were just too big. So we had to work out a filming schedule which would ensure we had enough litters to cover the scenes we needed."

The film used six adult dogs for the two leads and more than 200 puppies for the 99 other Dalmations. The high-energy animals were trained to respond to special commands and sounds, with a combination of praise and food treats. Most of the 200 were used as background pups, but six had their own special on-screen presence: Wizzer (two black ears);

Two-Tone (one black ear); Lucky (highly spotted); Dipstick (black tail); Jewel (a necklace of spots); and Fidget (one blue eye). Because several puppies played the same character, markings were added or taken away by a make-up artist using harmless vegetable dyes.

Not all of the puppies were real. "The logistics behind filming 99 puppies along with their parents is just mind boggling," said visual effects supervisor Michael Owens. For those mind boggling scenes, the production team turned to George Lucas's Industrial Light and Magic. They created a three-dimensional, digital, computer dog image that could be replicated to make multiple pups, each with its own distinctive markings. In the scene in which the puppies follow a sheep dog through a snowy farm, all the dogs are computer images.

Whether the dogs were computer images or the real thing, movie goers had spots before their eyes and couldn't get enough of the pervasive pups. Audiences swelled theaters, and *101 Dalmations* grossed $46 million, house breaking, as it were, the record for a five-day Thanksgiving opening.

LEADING A DOG'S LIFE

Lazing around most of the time, running through the house occasionally, and hitting the food bowl regularly are the usual characteristics of dogs belonging to television families. Leading a dog's life on TV isn't bad at all, as evidenced by these canine stars from hit television series.

Dreyfuss

When *Empty Nest* spun off from *The Golden Girls* in 1988, Miami pediatrician and recent widower Harry Weston (Richard Mulligan) confronted living alone with only his big, disobedient dog Dreyfuss for company. A mix of St. Bernard and golden retriever, Dreyfuss caused his share of trouble for Weston but helped the physician to remember that "life goes on." Dreyfuss was portrayed by look-alike canines Bear and Julio. The dog had his own problems when the household grew to include Weston's adult daughters: divorced and depressed Carol (Dinah Manoff) and clear-thinking police officer Barbara (Kristy McNichol). Next-door-neighbor Charley (David Leisure) was a lecherous sponge whose frequent visits shouldn't have happened to a dog.

Tramp

Another widower with a family dog was Steve Douglas (Fred MacMurray) on the long-running series, *My Three Sons* (1960–1972). In addition to Steve, the all-male household included his sons Mike (Tim Considine); Robbie (Don Grady); Chip (Stanley Livingston); grandfather Michael Francis "Bub" O'Casey (William Frawley); and the family pet, Tramp. Later, Ernie Thompson (Barry Livingston) and Uncle Charley O'Casey (William Demarest) joined the Douglas family. Through six seasons, as cast members came and went, Tramp remained a constant source of cheer and comfort. Trained by Frank Inn, Tramp was a four-

Tramp with Stanley Livingston, Fred MacMurray, Don Grady, William Demarest, and Barry Livingston. (*Archive Photos*)

time PATSY Award winner, capturing the honor from 1961 through 1964.

Jasper

The series *Bachelor Father* (1957–1962) featured yet another type of family arrangement. Handsome, wealthy Hollywood attorney Bentley Gregg (John Forsythe) was a much-sought-after bachelor, living in Beverly Hills with his niece Kelly (Noreen Corcoran) for whom he was a legal guardian, his houseboy Peter (Sammee Tong), and a large shaggy dog named Jasper. Jasper was awarded a PATSY in 1960 for his role in the series.

Ladadog

Jean Kerr's best-selling book about an unusual suburban family became a popular Doris Day movie and a television series with the same title, *Please Don't Eat the Daisies* (1965–1967). The family included Joan Nash (Patricia Crowley), a writer who hated housework and cooking; her husband Jim (Mark Miller), an English professor at Ridgemont College; their four sons, including a set of twins—Kyle (Kim Tyler), Joel (Brian Nash), Tracey (Joe Fithian), and Trevor (Jeff Fithian); and Ladadog, a 150-pound English sheep dog, played by Lord Nelson. For his role, Lord Nelson captured a PATSY Award in 1966.

Smiley

Hazel's (1961–66) household included George Baxter (Don DeFore), a successful corporate attorney; his wife Dorothy (Whitney Blake); their son Harold (Bobby Buntrock); their meddlesome, know-it-all housekeeper Hazel (Shirley Booth), and the Baxter's shaggy dog, Smiley. In 1965, Smiley, Harold, and Hazel moved to the household of George's brother, Steve Baxter, a real estate agent (Ray Fulmer); his wife Barbara (Lynn Borden); and their daughter Susie (Julia Benjamin). Smiley kept his sunny side up for five seasons with the various Baxters and the inimitable Hazel.

Earnest

The snoozing family pet on *Dave's World* (debuted 1993, CBS), starring Harry Anderson as a goofball humor columnist, was a bloodhound named Samantha. Before becoming a television star, Sam had an eight-year career as a rescue dog, then broke into the biz with a role in the 1993 film, *Amos 'n' Andrew*.

DUKE

Loose Skin Was His Claim To Fame

Old Ring on *The Tennessee Ernie Ford Show* (1956–1961), Old Blue in *No Time for Sergeants* (1958), and Duke on *The Beverly Hillbillies* (1962–1972) was a blood hound aptly named Stretch because of his over abundance of loose skin. "He was quite a dog," according to trainer Frank Inn. "He didn't do too much fancy stuff, but we trained him to do what old hounds do—lay around and sleep."

Stretch had the role of Old Ring, Tennessee Ernie Ford's dog, for five years on the NBC program. Inn recalled that one classic gag called for Ford to come out on stage with Stretch and mention to the audience that Old Ring was the smartest dog that had ever been. To demonstrate the dog's intelligence, Ford would command the dog to get the rabbit that was out in the audience. "Old Ring would just sit there or stand there, and then finally he would just lay down," Inn recalled. Ford would then say that that showed just how smart Old Ring was: The dog knew that there wasn't a rabbit in the audience.

"On *The Beverly Hillbillies*, all he had to do was just lay there. With his real loose skin, we could fix it so when he lay down, the skin would fall right over his eyes. You couldn't even see them," Inn said. Stretch

Louis Nye and Donna Douglas (Elly Mae) pamper Duke on an episode of *The Beverly Hillbillies.* (*Archive Photos*)

worked on *The Beverly Hillbillies* for about six years. "He got so old that I had to get a younger blood hound that looked like him to take his place," Inn said. "Nobody ever knew the difference. The only difference was that the younger blood hound never did have all the loose skin that Stretch had. The younger one had loose skin, but Stretch overdid it with loose skin."

EDDIE

He Stares Because He Cares

The "pet peeve" of Seattle radio talk-show host Dr. Frasier Crane is the presence of his father's dog, Eddie, on the couch, on the chair, just about anywhere in the psychiatrist's luxury apartment. But what *really* gets to Frasier is that stare. And audiences love it. The

Frasier (Kelsey Grammer) finds Eddie's stare discon-
certing. (*NBC/Everett Collection*)

scene-stealing Jack Russell terrier adept at unnerving the pompous Dr. Crane on NBC's Emmy-winning comedy *Frasier* (debuted 1993) has become the hippest, hottest canine in prime time.

Eddie, who's real name is Moose, began life in more modest circumstances. In his early years, he was a house pet in Orlando, Florida, until he drove his owner crazy with the super charged energy associated with the breed. His owner put him up for adoption. With a new owner, he moved to Los Angeles and began funneling his attention-getting hyperactivity into acting. A spot in a Louisiana State lottery commercial launched his career and landed him a supporting role on Kelsey Grammer's post-*Cheers* show, *Frasier*. The rest, as they say, is history.

Moose receives hundreds of fan letters a week, eats like a king—his favorite tidbits include home-cooked chicken, stew beef, and hot dogs—and enjoys the other perks that go along with stardom. "Moose gets recognized when we go out, but it's not out of control," said his trainer Mathilde De Cagny. "He doesn't have to wear sunglasses or anything."

According to De Cagny, Moose works well with the other cast members, especially Grammer. Frasier's grumpy persona notwithstanding, Grammer willingly assists the trainer by giving Moose cues or rewards during rehearsals or filming.

Moose remains single-minded in his quest to become a better actor. "He knows when it's time to be focused and rehearse, and he knows when it's time to play," De Cagny said. "He understands his limits. He knows he can tire himself out and lose his concentration."

But as long as Moose maintains that stare, the concentration of television viewers will be locked on *Frasier*.

"THE NAME IS FANG . . . FANG THE DOG"

He didn't have a shoe with a hidden phone, and would you believe he never had to use the infamous Cone of Silence. But trust me on this one, Chief, Agent K-13, also known as Fang, was C.O.N.T.R.O.L.'s incompetent canine operative on the situation comedy, *Get Smart* (1965–1970), a series that spoofed the popular James Bond movies.

Don Adams starred as the bumbling Maxwell Smart, Agent 86 for C.O.N.T.R.O.L., an international spy organization. His assistant was beautiful, brainy Agent 99 (Barbara Feldon). Each week they battled their K.A.O.S. enemies with an assortment of undercover oddballs, including The Chief (Edward Platt), Max's befuddled superior; Admiral Harold

Harmon Hargrade (William Schallert), former C.O.N.T.R.O.L. chief who fell into a coma-like sleep at critical moments; Agent 13 (Dave Ketchum), who hid in water fountains, clocks, and mailboxes; Hymie (Dick Gautier), a C.O.N.T.R.O.L. robot; and Agent K-13 (Fang, a mixed Briard), C.O.N.T.R.O.L.'s dog agent.

First featured in the pilot episode, Fang, Max, and 99 battled K.A.O.S.'s blackmailing Mr. Big (Michael Dunn), who threatened to use the Inthermo Ray unless C.O.N.T.R.O.L. paid $100 million. Fang, Max, and 99 discovered Mr. Big hiding out in a fake garbage scow and foiled his dastardly plot.

Through the first season, Fang tried to avoid engaging in derring-do in these episodes:

In "School Days," after it has been determined that a K.A.O.S. agent has infiltrated C.O.N.T.R.O.L.'s spy school, Fang and Max go undercover as students, and 99 poses as an instructor. Fang excels at the curriculum while Max fails every test he is given. At the end, the K.A.O.S. infiltrator is exposed, and Fang saves the day by blowing out the flame on the fuse of the dynamite.

For "Double Agent," Max is assigned to become an alcoholic, has-been agent in a ploy to have K.A.O.S. recruit him. To make his act convincing, Max alienates Fang, who leaves him. Now Fang-less, Max is recruited by K.A.O.S., and his first assignment is to kill 99.

In "I'm Only Human," Fang's poor attitude, including fleeing from danger and laying down on the job, caused him to be retired from C.O.N.T.R.O.L. Max convinces the Chief to reinstate Fang for one last mission: sending him undercover to a K.A.O.S. kennel. The kennel has been brainwashing pets to kill their owners. Fang is brainwashed by K.A.O.S., and the evil-doers black out Fang's Dog Collar Cam, a mini-television camera hidden in his collar, which lures Max into a trap.

Fang was forced to leave *Get Smart* during the second season. According to executive producer Leonard Stern, although the dog had a great personality, Fang would not respond to commands, so he was written out of the series. (The old when-you-can't-teach-an-old-dog-new-tricks-you-hand-the-Briard-his-walking-papers trick.) Content to collect his dog-biscuit pension and chase an occasional cat, Fang often wished he could be back in the action, biting bad guys, enduring heinous torture, saving the world from the domination of evil. Would you believe playing with his toy duck and one of Max's slippers? Would you believe sauntering through the small swinging door in the Chief's office for a snooze? And he'd be loving it.

FREMONT

Good Ol' Mister Wilson's Dog

Fremont, the cairn terrier who played George Wilson's pet in the series *Dennis the Menace* started his show biz career on *I Love Lucy*, as Little Ricky's puppy. According to trainer Frank Inn, the dog appeared on *I Love Lucy* about a dozen times, mostly as an atmosphere animal.

Those appearances probably attracted the attention of the production team casting the role of Fremont for *Dennis the Menace* (1959–1963). The team contracted for the now-adult

Who is that doggie in the window? Fremont works his magic on Frank Sinatra and Kim Novak in *Pal Joey*.

dog to become the pet of Mr. Wilson, Dennis Mitchell's next-door neighbor.

Jay North, who played Dennis, was a typical kid who loved dogs, and he was crazy about Fremont, according to Frank Inn. Unfortunately, the studio mother who was in charge of North wouldn't let the child play with the dog, although Inn encouraged the other cast members to play with Fremont. Fremont had the role for two seasons, but during that time he didn't do anything important or stand out in any way: He was just Fremont, a little bit naughty but mostly nice.

Almost every actor yearns for bigger and better projects, and Fremont's break came when Columbia Pictures was preparing the 1957 motion picture *Pal Joey* with Rita Hayworth, Frank Sinatra, and Kim Novak. Thanks to an almost look-alike dog named Snuffy, Fremont landed the part on that picture.

The studio wanted an unknown dog for the role, one that had been rescued from an animal shelter, trained, and made into a star. At the time, Inn had a partner who had an old, rheumatic dog named Snuffy. "That dog could do about anything," Inn said. Rather than trying to find a dog from a shelter and training it, Inn and his partner brought Snuffy to the animal shelter, left him there, then returned several days later to "adopt" him.

The studio sponsored a huge reception at a downtown Hollywood restaurant where animal trainers could show their dogs for the role in *Pal Joey*. Part of the audition included having each dog eat a bagel. "We took this dog that was already fairly well trained and trained it to pick up a bagel and dip it into a bowl of soup then lay the bagel down and eat the soft part of it," Inn said.

Forty dogs appeared at the reception, which was covered by the Hollywood press corps, and Snuffy won the role. "The press thought it was remarkable that this dog had come out of the animal shelter," Inn said, and reporters wrote stories attesting to the fact that it was possible to teach an old dog new tricks.

Snuffy was indeed an old dog, and Inn and his partner did not think he would be able to do the work required for the motion picture. Snuffy was the same size and type as the younger Fremont, the only difference was their coloring: Snuffy was blonde while Fremont was reddish gray. "We bleached Fremont," according to Inn, "and you couldn't tell them apart." So Fremont had his chance at movie stardom, while Snuffy became Fremont's double dog in *Pal Joey*.

GOING APE OVER TELEVISION

From the 1950s with the antics of J. Fred Muggs through the 1990s with Marcel from *Friends*, television audiences have enjoyed the monkeyshines of many an ape on television series. To celebrate prime time stars like them, here is a primer of particularly playful primates:

Bingo the Chimp

Bingo cavorted with Bud and Lou on 26 episodes of *The Abbott and Costello Show*, syndicated from 1952 to 1953. The boys played unemployed actors rooming together in a boarding house. Bingo was their pet. Unfortunately, Bingo bit the boss—Lou—and was given his walking papers. The remaining 26 episodes were Bingo-less.

The Marquis Chimps

Elinore and Walter Hathaway were "parents" of Charlie, Enoch, and Cindy. *The Hathaways* (1961–1962) were an unusual family because the "children" were chimpanzees and a show-business act to boot. Elinore (Peggy Cass) acted as their mom, manager, and unofficial booking agent, finding them gigs riding bicycles and making faces. Her husband Walter (Jack Weston) was a real estate agent who often wondered if his wife loved the chimps more than she loved him. Their suburban neighbors had their own ideas about the lovably wacky couple and the "kids" next door.

Debbie

When the spaceship *Jupiter II* blasted off for a five-year voyage to explore a planet in the Alpha Centauri star system, the Robinson family had no idea that an evil stowaway saboteur (Jonathan Harris) would tinker with the control system and cause them all to become *Lost in Space* (1965–1968). As the weekly adventures unfolded, Professor John Robinson (Guy Williams); his wife Maureen (June Lockhart); their children Judy (Marta Kristen), Will (Billy Mummy), and Penny (Angela Cartwright); and their pilot Don West (Mark Goddard) met strange and fanciful life forms. One such life form was a monkey-like creature called a Space Bloop, and because of its resemblance to an Earth chimpanzee, the Robinson family adopted it as a pet named Jenny. Jenny was played by Debbie, a versatile chimp. She was also a series regular on *The Beverly Hillbillies* (1962–1972) as Cousin Bess, one of Elly May's "critters." She co-starred with Tonga on *Lancelot Link, Secret Chimp*. Debbie played Mata Hairi.

Tonga

Tonga was the star of a unique television series that featured no human beings among the cast members. In *Lancelot Link, Secret Chimp* (1970–1972), Tonga played Lancelot

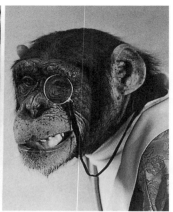

Lancelot Link, Mata Hairi, and Baron Von Burcher were the hip cast of *Lancelot Link, Secret Chimp*. (*Archive Photos*)

Link, a counter-espionage agent for A.P.E. (Agency to Prevent Evil), headed by Commander Darwin. The goal of A.P.E. was to defeat the international organization C.H.U.M.P. (Criminal Headquarters for Underground Master Plan), its leader Baron Von Butcher, and his assistant Creator. Assisting Lance in this quest was the beautiful secret agent, Mata Hairi. Each week, Lance and Mata donned disguises then rode motorcycles, drove boats, and rode horses to halt C.H.U.M.P.'s attempt at world domination. All of the actors were chimpanzees except for Commander Darwin, who was an orangutan.

The trainer behind the *Lancelot Link* lunacy was Frank Inn. The show's producers wanted a large chimp to play their hero, so Inn found Tonga, a nine-year-old chimpanzee who at 140 pounds was twice the size of a normal chimp. Because of the danger and unpredictability of apes, Inn used a trainer for each animal.

The chimps had to behave like people, so Inn concocted clever illusions to give this impression. For example, when Lance hopped on a motorcycle, the vehicle was actually a motor scooter. When Lance drove a boat, he merely held the wheel while a crew member hidden under the wheel steered the vessel. When Lance and Mata rode their mounts, the horses were of the miniature variety used in circuses. The animals "talked" in each episode: Trainers cued the chimps to open and close their mouths in sync with the words written in the script. Human actors dubbed in the voices later.

Master trainer Frank Inn is especially proud of his work on *Lancelot Link*. As he commented, "It was much harder to do than it looked, because chimps are so hard to deal with."

Bear

Young, good-looking trucker Billie Joe "B.J." McKay (Greg Evigan) logged many miles in his red-and-white rig, traveling around the country with his pet chimpanzee, Bear. *B.J. and the Bear* (1979–1981) followed their assorted adventures hauling freight and fighting corruption in rural Georgia during the first season and in Los Angeles during the second season. When B.J. established his trucking business, Bear Enterprises, he hired seven young, beautiful women truckers (including a pair of identical twins). Although romance was always just around the next curve, B.J. kept close to his "best friend Bear."

HOOCH

Can This Dog Make an Entrance, or What?

In the 1989 film *Turner and Hooch*, small-town police investigator Scott Turner (Tom Hanks) must solve a murder with the help of a sloppy, slobbering French mastiff named Hooch. The dog wrecks Scott's house and turns his compulsively ordered life completely upside down. Turner first meets Hooch in a screen moment that is pure movie magic:

Turner arrives at the harborside home of Amos Reed (John McIntire) to investigate Reed's complaint of something "fishy" going on at the nearby seafood processing plant. Through the gate of the chain-link fence guarding the dock, Turner yells to Reed, announcing his presence.

"Let me get a leash on him," Reed calls.

"Yeah. Do that. Please."

Detective Turner's (Tom Hanks) life is turned upside down by Hooch. (*Archive Photos/fotos international*)

Clutching a muffin, Turner passes through the gate then walks cautiously toward the junk-yard boat. Suddenly, in slow motion, and to the strains of "Thus Spake Zarathustra," a massive dog bounds through a window, runs down a set of steps, and gambols along the walkway toward Turner.

"Hey, I brought you a muffin, boy. Here's a muffin for you. See the muffin. See the muffin, Hooch. It's a muffin for Hooch," Turner nervously backs up as the dog gets closer. The dog propels himself at Turner who shouts, "I BROUGHT A MUFFIN FOR YOU!" The dog knocks Turner on his back, the muffin becomes airborne, and Hooch sinks his teeth into the officer's throat, pining him to the walkway.

Reed hurries toward the confrontation and manages to pull Hooch off Turner. Reed helps the angry officer to his feet, apologizing for not being able to get the leash on the dog and making sure that Turner is okay. Reed looks at Turner's neck. "Why, he didn't even break the skin. Well, this dog loves you, boy. Let's go on up to the house, and we'll all have a cookie."

Hooch passes the fallen muffin and gobbles it in one bite—paper wrapper and all.

According to Hooch's trainer, Clint Rowe, the film's director Roger Spottiswoode was amazed when he viewed the dailies of this scene. "We went back and shot more footage," Rowe said. He recalled that Spottiswoode, with tongue firmly in cheek, said: "Hooch's entrance is going to be like Omar Sharif's entrance in *Lawrence of Arabia*." The music, from *2001: A Space Odyssey*, was used in the rough cut of the film but worked so well it was left in.

Hooch, whose real name was Beasly, had a good off-screen relationship with actor Tom Hanks. Rowe said: "I got a letter from Tom after the film saying that one of the nicest things about working on the show was the dog." And could that dog make an entrance!

LAWRENCE

Symbol of the Hartford Insurance Company

Remember the logo of the Hartford Insurance Company—a majestic, mature, fully-racked elk standing on a mountain? The animal responsible for bringing that logo to life in television commercials was not an elk at all but a European red deer named Lawrence.

When the company decided to make a foray into television commercials with a live logo, they contacted noted animal trainer, Ralph Helfer. Helfer did not have an elk in his collection and wasn't sure he could locate a tame one. (Elks are notorious for being dangerously unpredictable.)

Helfer scoured zoos and animal compounds throughout the United States and Canada and learned that the European red deer resembles an elk and that a small zoo in Florida had such a deer.

When Helfer traveled to the zoo, he found a large animal with an eight-point rack. According to Helfer, "He was heavy in body, with a thick, reddish coat, and he appeared to weigh at least 500 pounds. He so strongly resembled the elk in the logo that we decided he would be the perfect animal to represent Hartford Insurance." Helfer named the deer Lawrence and trained him with affection—petting, hand-feeding, brushing, gentle handling—and with the reward system.

The commercials were shot in the Angeles Crest mountains of southern California. Lawrence wasn't required to perform any stunts, but the trick was to get him to act naturally—climb a hill, stop on a mark, look out over the valley, and then move on—on cue. That took some ingenuity on Helfer's part.

Helfer and four handlers were on hand for filming. At the director's call for action, Helfer opened the corral in which Lawrence was housed. A handler near the camera called to Lawrence, shook a bucket of oat-and-barley mix, and watched as the deer walked up the hill toward him. When Lawrence reached the mark where he was to stop, another handler carrying a large sheet of metal and a stick bounded out of the forest 100 yards away and ran across an open field, pounding on the metal sheet with the stick. Hearing the racket, Lawrence stopped and looked in the direction of the noise. Once his curiosity was satisfied, Lawrence continued walking over the hill and reached the handler with the bucket of grain.

The commercial was a success, and the Hartford Insurance Company signed Lawrence to a long-term contract to make other commercials. In some of those commercials, Lawrence walked down a residential street; in others he walked by a house under construction. So impressive were the commercials that Lawrence earned PATSY Awards in 1975 and 1977.

LEO

The Roaring Symbol of Metro-Goldwyn-Mayer

Thousands of films, from *Gone With the Wind* to *Jailhouse Rock* have been introduced by the roar of the most famous lion in moviedom: Leo, the symbol of Metro-Goldwyn-Mayer.

Film producer Samuel Goldwyn sought an instantly recognizable symbol for his studio, Goldwyn Pictures Corporation, incorporated in 1916. He consulted advertising expert Philip Goodman who asked his new employee Howard Dietz to develop the corporate logo. Dietz created a logo featuring an illustration of the King of

(*Archive Photos*)

the Beasts in full-body profile with the Latin phrase "*Ars Gratia Artis*" (Art for Art's Sake) in a crest of film above the lion. The words "Goldwyn Pictures Corporation" in large letters were superimposed over the lion logo. As Dietz recalled, "I got the idea from the laughing lion decoration in the college comic *The Jester*. The lion used in the magazine was a symbol of Columbia University [which Dietz had attended], which in turn was taken from the lion on the crest of Kings College. That's powerful lineage enough for a film company."

The film company obtained its first live Leo from an animal farm in Gilette, Pennsylvania, and used the lion to promote its films. The image of this lion was used in all Goldwyn movies released after 1921.

In 1924, Metro Pictures, Goldwyn Pictures Corporation, and Louis B. Mayer Productions merged to form Metro-Goldwyn-Mayer. Leo was kept as the focal point of the new company's logo, but the lion was shown full face rather than in profile. MGM obtained its own live lion in 1927, and in 1928 the roar of a lion named Pluto was recorded for the distinctive MGM trademark. Louis B. Mayer decided to use two fast roars, a pause, and then a third roar for a ferocious addition to the corporate identity. The first film introduced by Leo the Lion's roar was the 1928 movie *White Shadows in the South Seas*.

MGM's Leo went on the road for promotional appearances. In fact, as a publicity stunt in 1927 to coincide with Lindbergh's historic flight to Paris, MGM sent Leo on what would have been a nonstop airplane flight from California to New York. Unfortunately, the plane only flew as far as Arizona before it crashed in the Tonto Basin. Leo, an old lion with only one tooth, was lost for several days—making for wonderful publicity for the studio. After Leo was rescued, he was sent back on the road in his more usual method of touring the country—a three-truck entourage. One truck carried Leo's business manager, the second carted a calliope, and the third, with silver bars on the cage, was Leo's home away from home.

Since then, Leo has been played by other lions whose symbolic roar at the start of a film tells viewers that they are in for a wild time at the movies.

HE'S FINICKY! HE'S SARCASTIC! HE'S MORRIS!

In 1969 the advertising agency representing Star-Kist Foods, Inc. needed a cat for the television commercials they planned to promote 9-Lives cat food. Animal trainer Bob Martwick was given the task of finding a suitable animal. The animal that Martwick found was a fourteen-pound, salmon-orange tiger cat he named Lucky. Martwick thought the name perfectly suited the stray from the Hinsdale, Illinois, animal shelter—the cat was 20 minutes away from being put to sleep when Martwick adopted him.

When the trainer brought the cat to the ad agency, he found the staff huddled around a table, busily mapping out the cat food campaign and barely paying attention to Martwick's find. Apparently the cat couldn't stand not being the center of attention. He jumped onto the table, scattering documents and notes and making an impression that had the word "star" written all over it. That was the agency's "lucky" day, because before them sauntered the cat that would soon become Morris, the most recognized and celebrated pitch puss in the world of advertising.

After such a strong introduction, the agency decided to make Morris a star. As with most soon-to-be celebrities, the choice of a professional name was critical. Someone noticed that the configuration of tiger stripes on the cat's forehead formed the letter "M," and this inspired the selection of the name Morris. Once the name was chosen, Bob Martwick began training Morris not to perform tricks or stunts but to not budge even though his television "owner" called "Time for din-din, Morris." For Morris, the entree of choice was 9-Lives or nothing.

Filming the commercials with Morris was challenging for his directors. Voice-overs for the commercials—Morris's dialogue—were prepared in advance by a human actor. The job of the director was to photograph Morris with the appropriate facial expressions and body movements to accompany the dialogue. And directors who required multiple takes soon learned that Morris was not one to put up with such nonsense. While other cat actors might scratch, bite, howl, or run away when they had their fill of acting for the day, Morris didn't pull any such "hiss"-trionics." Instead Morris just calmly walked off the set.

Morris appeared in more than fifty 9-Lives television commercials, and his self-confident personality added to his audience appeal. Morris won a PATSY Award in 1973.

He was mobbed by fans at personal appearances across the country, and he received the full star treatment: traveling in limousines and staying in only the best hotels. He made a break into feature films, co-starring with Burt Reynolds in the 1973 film *Shamus*. Morris was featured on the television programs *Lifestyles of the Rich and Famous* and on *Good Morning, America*. And befitting the celebrity that he was, he also had his own press agent.

As Morris grew older, the advertising agency sought a look-alike cat as an eventual replacement for the 9-Lives' spokespuss. After a seven-year search, Morris II was discovered in a New England animal shelter and was groomed to step into some mighty big paw prints.

When Morris died in 1978, his obituary was carried on the major wire services, broadcast on television stations, and written up in newspapers around the country. To show respect for their late star, Star-Kist Foods, Inc. pulled their Morris commercials from the air for a mourning period of several days.

He was finicky, he was sarcastic, he was Morris! And the country loved him just the way he was.

NO "MOOSE"–TAKING MORTY

Viewers spotted him every week at the opening of the Emmy-Award-winning television series *Northern Exposure* (1990–1995)—the moose strolling the streets of Cicely, Alaska. A shy, retiring fellow, Morty made his presence known quietly so as not to disturb the quirky residents of the tiny tundra town, including Dr. Joel, Maurice, Maggie, Holling, Ed, Chris, Shelly, Marilyn, and Ruth-Anne, and then later Dr. and Mrs. Philip Capra. Morty's television stardom was unexpected, according to his caretaker, Charlie Robbins. And Robbins advised Morty to nix an appearance at the 1992 Emmy Awards. "I couldn't imagine [him] in Hollywood," Robbins said. "He'd rearrange some dentures if he got loose." A moose on the loose? Always in Cicely, but never in Tinseltown.

Morty was a member of a captive moose herd maintained for breeding purposes at the research station of Washington State University. He sired a number of offspring, including Melody and Matilda, born in 1993. Morty was part of a nutritional research program. Unfortunately, Morty died of inflammatory bowel disease, a condition that also affects people.

Northern Exposure, filmed in Roslyn, Washington, was not renewed for a seventh season; the last episode aired in July 1995. However, the series entered syndication in 1994, and fans can still see Morty in re-run heaven.

NIPPER

The RCA Dog

The dog listening to the cylinder phonograph is Nipper, the well-known symbol of RCA. What many people don't know is that Nipper was once a real dog.

A smooth-haired fox terrier, Nipper belonged to the brother of English artist Francis

(© *Thompson Consumer Electronics*)

Barraud in the 1890s. After his brother died, Barraud adopted Nipper and was amazed at the dog's behavior when the phonograph was played. The little dog stood transfixed in front of the machine with tilted head and cocked ears, listening intently. Inspired, Barraud painted a portrait of Nipper in that pose and titled the work "His Master's Voice."

Barraud offered the portrait to a cylinder manufacturer, but the company was not interested. However, a small phonograph manufacturer, the Gramophone Company, was intrigued, and Barraud sold the portrait to them. The visual image of the portrait was adopted by EMI Records Limited as their trademark, and EMI leased the symbol to RCA.

Nipper was first used in a magazine advertisement for an RCA Victrola and soon was a corporate symbol indelibly etched in the minds of millions. Nipper eventually appeared in television advertising, and a modern-day Nipper—complete with pups—continues the advertising tradition.

Nipper reached new heights of advertising—literally—when, in 1954, the W.L. Stansgaard Co. and Associates of Chicago built a 25 ½-foot-tall, 4-ton Nipper for the top of the RTA building on North Broadway in Albany, New York. A distributor of RCA electrical appliances, RTA had purchased the circa-1912 building and wanted an eye-catching emblem to grace the structure. This titanic terrier—the world's largest man-made dog—has a steel frame, a composite body, and a beacon on his ear to protect Nipper from low-flying aircraft. A familiar sight from downtown Albany streets, Nipper can be seen up to five miles away and has been called "the Statue of Liberty for advertising."

TEARS FOR OLD YELLER

The 1957 film *Old Yeller* was the first attempt by Disney Studios to film a story about a boy and his dog, and it was a heart-wrenching success.

Based on the novel by Fred Gipson, *Old Yeller* told the tale of a Texas farm family in 1869. Father Jim Coates (Fess Parker) embarks on a three-month cattle drive, leaving his fifteen-year-old son Travis (Tommy Kirk) in charge as the man of the house. Travis' younger brother Arliss (Kevin Corcoran) finds and adopts a stray yellow dog (played by Spike) that he names Old Yeller. Mother Katie Coates (Dorothy McGuire) encourages the friendship between the dog and her younger son. Soon Old Yeller has endeared himself to the whole family.

When Travis and Old Yeller go off to trap wild pigs, they become trapped by the vicious animals. Old Yeller fights off the attacking animals, but both Travis and Old Yeller return to the farm wounded. Once their wounds heal, Travis confines Old Yeller because the boy is fearful that the dog may have contracted rabies. Time passes, and Travis believes that the danger of rabies has passed. Old Yeller is reunited with the happy family.

Then, one day, Old Yeller turns extremely vicious for no apparent reason. Travis is shocked and realizes that the dog has indeed contracted rabies. Having no other alternative, Travis shoots the beloved animal.

When Jim Coates returns home to his family, he learns of all that transpired during his absence. He helps Travis deal with Old Yeller's death. After visiting the dog's grave, Travis adopts a puppy fathered by Old Yeller and sees the spirit of his old friend in the small puppy.

Only the most hard-hearted movie goer failed to weep when Old Yeller died. The heart breaking death

(*Archive Photos/Walt Disney Co.*)

scene was an inspired piece of acting by Spike. Spike was trained by Rudd Weatherwax, Lassie's trainer. For his role as Old Yeller, Spike won a PATSY Award in 1958.

Spike had a role in another children's tear-jerker, *Dog of Flanders* (1959), which starred David Ladd, Donald Crisp, and Theodore Bikel. This film told the story of Nello (David Ladd), a Dutch boy with an impossible dream of becoming a painter. He and his grandfather (Donald Crisp) make a meager living by delivering milk. One day they find a sickly dog (Spike), nurse him back to health, and make him their cart dog. After the grandfather dies, the boy and his dog are thrown out into the cold, cruel world. Finally, the pair is adopted by a painter (Theodore Bikel), proving that dreams can come true. Again, his heart-wrenching performance earned him a PATSY. Well done (sniff, sniff), Spike!

ROCKS AND DAPHNE

Look Who's Talking Now

The third entry in the *Look Who's Talking* series of films, 1993's *Look Who's Talking Now*, features a *Lady-and-the-Tramp*-type combo of Daphne (a standard poodle named Lilly with the voice of Diane Keaton) and Rocks (a mutt named Scrapper with the voice of Danny DeVito).

In the film, James (John Travolta) and Mollie (Kirstie Alley) are parents of six-year-old

Daphne (*left*) and Rocks. (*Archive Photos/TriStar Pictures/fotos international*)

Mikey (David Gallagher) and four-year-old Julie (Tabitha Lupien). James brings home a dog-pound mutt, Rocks, for Mikey at the same time that James's new boss (Lysette Anthony) foists her pedigreed poodle, Daphne, on the family. The differences between the two dogs cannot be more evident.

While Daphne enjoys daily "paw-dicures," Rocks devours designer shoes. Daphne teaches Rocks to sit; Rocks takes Daphne out on the town to experience running without a leash, rooting through garbage cans, and sloshing through mud. At the end of the film, Rocks becomes a hero, defending the family against vicious wolves.

Trainer Mark Watters characterized Lilly as being "goofy—kind of like a Valley Girl," while he characterized Scrapper as being "very sensitive" despite his casting as a tough guy. Scrapper's sensitive side is illustrated by his preference for chewing only designer shoes. No ordinary slippers or sneakers for this boy, which leads audiences to conclude, despite evidence to the contrary, that Scrapper *does* indeed know the meaning of the word "heel."

SADDLE UP

Horses, Heroes, and Sidekicks

What would a Western be without heroes saddling up their horses and riding along sagebrush trails with their loyal sidekicks. Here are five famous Western pairs from the thrilling days of yesteryear.

The Adventure of Wild Bill Hickok

This television show, syndicated from 1951–1958, featured Guy Madison as frontier marshal Wild Bill Hickok and Andy Devine as his sidekick. Madison rode the horse Buckshot while Devine rode Joker.

Annie Oakley

From 1953 to 1956, Gail Davis starred as the American markswoman, Annie Oakley, and the series featured her adventures in the 1860s West. Her sidekick was her brother Tagg (Jimmy Hawkins). Davis rode Target, and Hawkins rode Pixie.

The Cisco Kid

Duncan Renaldo portrayed the Cisco Kid, a Mexican cowboy, on this series from 1950 to 1956. His pinto horse was named Diablo. The Cisco Kid's sidekick was Pancho (Leo Carrillo), and his golden palomino was named Loco.

Gunsmoke

From 1955 to 1975, audiences followed the stories of U.S. Marshal Matt Dillon (James Arness) as he tried to maintain the peace in Dodge City, Kansas, in the 1880s. His sidekick was Festus Haggen (Ken Curtis). While Arness rode a horse named Marshall, Curtis had to be content with an ornery yet faithful mule named Ruth.

The Range Rider

Jock Mahoney starred as the Range Rider, galloping through the Wild West on his horse Rawhide. Rider's young sidekick was played by Dick Jones, who called his mount Lucky. The series ran from 1951 to 1953.

LEAPIN' LIZARDS! IT'S SANDY

The girl with the white eyes and her dog, Sandy, originated in the funny papers. *Little Orphan Annie* debuted in the *New York Daily News* in 1924, and Annie and Sandy were together through thick and thin as a comic strip for more than fifty years. Annie and Sandy made a giant leap from the comics pages to theatrical stages as a musical and then to the silver screen as a major motion picture.

Annie began as a local production of the Goodspeed Opera House in Connecticut where Bill Berloni worked as an actor and carpenter. As a favor to the producer, Berloni agreed to locate a dog for the role of Sandy. Berloni visited a half-dozen humane societies and found a medium-sized, terrier-mix dog cowering in the corner of his cage at the Newington, Connecticut, Humane Society. Berloni paid $8 to adopt the dog, who was scheduled to be put to sleep the next day.

Working in theater meant that Sandy had to hit his mark the first time and every time. To accustom the dog to performing on stage, Berloni brought Sandy to the theater after hours and allowed the dog to become comfortable on stage. Berloni trained Sandy to hit his mark by placing a small piece of bologna on stage. He taught Sandy to find the meat, stand there, look around, then run offstage.

Annie made it to Broadway in 1977. Sandy performed one show a night, plus a matinee and an evening show on weekends, and *Annie* became a hit, winning a multitude of awards, grossing more than $200 million, and running for more than 2,000 performances. Sandy became Broadway's number one animal star and in 1978 was honored with The Craven Award, recognition given by the American Humane Association to animals specializing in stunt work. Leapin' Lizards!

SASSY, CHANCE, AND SHADOW

Homeward Bound: The Incredible Journey

Shadow, Chance, and Sassy. (*Archive Photos/ Walt Disney Co.*)

Filming *Homeward Bound: The Incredible Journey* (1993), the story of three household pets—Sassy, Chance, and Shadow—on a mountainous trek to be reunited with their owners, was an incredible job for animal coordinator Joe Camp of Jungle Exotics. Although the production team had discovered Himalayan Sassy in Camp's office (see profile of Salty), they spent a month looking at nearly 140 dogs for the roles of Chance, the American bull dog, and Shadow, the golden retriever.

Having found the lead animals and their various stand-ins, Camp then had the task of coordinating their training. Rather than working with the animals in groups, trainers worked with the animals individually. Dogs were trained to respond to hand signals and voice commands, while cats were trained with a buzzer sound.

"All of the animals were represented by teams," Camp said. The lead dog playing Chance was a ten-week-old puppy named Rattler. His double was Be, a small female, and the dogs Tex and UFO provided their expertise in running.

The lead dog playing the older dog, Shadow, was Ben, an eight-year-old prematurely gray dog. He was doubled by Molly, who did most of the required swimming. Tyler acted as the running dog, and Montgomery was the stand-in for swimming and leaping into the water after Sassy.

Tiki was the lead cat for Sassy, and she had seven doubles, including Remington, Curly, and Chubby, who went on to do double work for Tiki playing Salty on the television series, *Caroline in the City*.

Motivators for the animals included toys, affection, and food, especially pieces of hot dog and liver. In fact, one person on the set had the sole responsibility of cooking liver throughout the day.

To convince the cat to follow the dogs, a radio-powered, remote-controlled buzzer was hidden underneath the dogs' collars. The sound of the buzzer told the cat to follow the dogs and be rewarded. For the animals' reunion scene at the end of the film, the script called for the cat to give the dog a big hug. That's what it looked like on the screen. What happened during filming was that the cat pulled a piece of meat from under the dog's collar. Incredible, yet true.

SPIKE

Straight Monkey to Jim Carrey

Spike in both *Ace Ventura* movies is a male, white-front Capuchin monkey named Binx. He had his hands full being the straight monkey to the wild-man pet detective played by Jim Carrey. In *Ace Ventura: Pet Detective* (1994), Carrey solves the kidnapping of Snowflake, the Miami Dolphins' mascot and the subsequent disappearance of the Dolphins' star quarterback, Dan Marino. In *Ace Ventura: When Nature Calls* (1995), Carrey travels to Africa to find a white bat and to prevent a war between two rival tribes. That's quite a bit for a small monkey to support. So after each film, Binx de-stressed by hanging out in trees, swinging from branches, and popping back a few bananas. Ah, the good life.

SPOT

Star Trek: The Next Generation

Spot, android Data's (Brent Spiner) outer space pussy cat on *Star Trek: The Next Generation* (1987–1994) was played by not one but two talented feline look-alikes, Brandy and Monster. According to owner Rob Bloch, "Brandy does most of the lying-around scenes, and Monster does most of the jumping and running." However, Brandy has more skill than those lying-around scenes might suggest. Brandy can beg, wave, and sleep on command.

Spot's most unique contribution to the crew of the twenty-fourth-century starship *Enterprise* was providing the clue that a substance in amniotic fluid would cure a virus causing all of the ship's life forms to de-evolve to a previous life form. Spot herself reverted to a lizard, but her newly born kittens were fine, leading to the intergalactic biological revelation. Once amniotic fluid taken from a gestational crew member was added to the ship's air system, all advanced to their current life forms. Well done, Spot.

SYN

That Darn Cat

The 1965 Disney film, *That Darn Cat* tells the hilarious story of a Siamese cat named D.C. (for Darn Cat) owned by Patti Randall (Hayley Mills). A wristwatch around the cat's neck is the only clue to a bank robbery and kidnapping. D.C. leads F.B.I. agent Zeke Kelso (Dean Jones) on a merry chase down alleys, through a drive-in theater, and under fences until the agent plants a transmitter under the cat's collar and tails the cat to the kidnappers' apartment. D.C. helps collar the crooks by tripping one of them on the stairs.

Syn, the Siamese cat who starred in *That Darn Cat* had also starred in *The Incredible Journey* (1963). For that film, trainer Bill Koehler used the cue of a large swinging sheep bell to prompt Syn to perform the script's outdoor tricks and stunts. He felt that a cue from a small buzzer would work better on the interior set for *That Darn Cat*. But, the cat would need weeks of training to become adjusted to the buzzer. Would the cat respond to a recording of the bell? Koehler tried, using a tape recording of the bell broadcast though a two-inch-wide speaker. Koehler smeared meat on the speaker for added incentive, released Syn from his cord-activated release box, and the cat went directly to the speaker. Koehler was thrilled. Syn's reaction meant that he could be cued using a speaker placed unobtrusively on the set, under clothing, behind a lamp, or underneath furniture.

Koehler's next concern was Syn's relationship with star Hayley Mills. He needn't have worried. Mills was an animal lover, and she went out of her way to carry Syn in her arms during rehearsals and to cradle the cat in her lap when relaxing between scenes. Syn responded by kneading her arm with his front paws, licking her wrist, and pushing his head against her neck and chin.

"It was very easy to believe that Syn was Hayley Mills' Darn Cat," Koehler said. The American Humane Association thought so, too. The organization honored Syn with a PATSY Award in 1966 for his work in *That Darn Cat*.

Tiger brings up the rear of the Brady Bunch.
(*Archive Photos*)

A VERY BRADY TIGER

Several dogs played the role of Tiger in the television series, *The Brady Bunch* (1969-1974), the story of a blended family and their housekeeper. Acquired from an animal shelter, Tiger #1 was used in the pilot episode that sold the series. When the series went into production, Lou

Schumacher was hired to provide the animal action and located Tiger #2. Trainer Karl Lewis Miller trained Tiger #2, who appeared in two episodes, then Miller left to train animals for a motion picture. Another trainer took over the training duties of Tiger #2, but tragically, the dog was hit by a truck during a walk. On short notice, Tiger #3 had to be located. This Tiger was not as well trained as the previous Tigers and was soon replaced by Tiger #4, who was replaced by Tiger #5, who was replaced by Tiger #6. According to Karl Lewis Miller, "eventually the studio began using the dog less and less because it was too much hassle, so many principal actors, so many kids that they had to do coverage on, and they just couldn't give more time to the dog in the story." Tiger was a mixed Hungarian sheepdog.

TONY THE WONDER HORSE

The Roaring '20s were more spirited thanks to cowboy actor and stunt man Tom Mix and his wonder horse, Tony. Together the pair thrilled silent-film audiences by leaping from tall cliffs, scaling rocky canyons, and escaping from dangerous fires through more than 50 motion pictures.

A real-life cowboy from the rodeo and Wild West show circuit, Mix began his film career in 1914 with the Selig Polyscope Company. His rodeo horse, Old Blue, made the transition to film work in the two- and three-reel Western shorts in which he and Mix starred, but the horse died in 1917. When Mix moved to the Fox Studios that same year, he acquired the fearless Tony.

Mix, who never let the truth get in the way of a good story, offered over the years several variations of Tony's discovery. In one version, Mix was tooling along the streets of Hollywood in his new Stutz when he noticed a magnificent chestnut-colored horse with white hind socks pulling a vegetable cart. Mix stopped and asked the Italian vegetable peddler how much he wanted for the horse. The street merchant hesitated, so Mix pulled out a wad of ten-dollar bills and peeled them off one by one until the peddler agreed to the sale. After the bargain was struck, Mix asked the merchant for the horse's name but was told he didn't have one. Mix then asked the peddler for *his* name; when told that the man's name was Tony, Mix decided it was a good name for the horse.

In the eleven years that Mix and Tony worked for Fox Studios, they became the top cowboy-horse team in silent films, eclipsing even veterans such as William S. Hart and his horse, Fritz. Tony astounded audiences by untying knots with this teeth, running for help when Mix was in a fix, and galloping alongside speeding locomotives so that Mix could jump from the train into the saddle. Lovers of danger, Mix and Tony were unstoppable in front of the camera and only used doubles when forced by the studio.

By 1928, the popularity of Westerns was declining, sound films were on the horizon, and Fox Studios declined to renew Mix's contract. Mix moved to Joseph P. Kennedy's F.B.O. Company, but the six silent films he and Tony made there were considered inferior to their earlier pictures. Undaunted, Mix and Tony toured the country for a number of years as a successful circus act and then returned to film work at Universal Pictures in early 1932.

By this time, Tony was twenty-three years old, and the years were starting to show. In October 1932, while filming a sequence in the Mojave Desert, Tony slipped and tumbled down a five-foot embankment, rolled over on his side, and pinned Mix underneath him. While Tony was more scared than hurt, Mix was knocked unconscious and injured his right leg and side. The pair retired from film work in December 1932.

The final fadeout for Mix came on October 10, 1940, when he was killed in an automobile accident heading to Phoenix on an Arizona highway. On the same date two years later, Tony joined Mix in the heavenly corral.

Won Ton Ton

The Dog Who Spoofed Hollywood

The 1976 cult classic *Won Ton Ton: The Dog Who Saved Hollywood* spoofs two venerable Hollywood institutions: the film *A Star Is Born* and the film star Rin Tin Tin. Set in 1920s Hollywood, the plot followed the adventures of a lost Alsatian dog who becomes a movie star, suffers the ups and downs of fame, and is finally reunited with his mistress. Human stars included Bruce Dern, Madeline Kahn, Art Carney, Phil Silvers, Teri Garr, and Ron Leibman. The canine star of the film was a German shepherd named Augustus Von Schumacher—affectionately called Gus—owned by animal supplier Lou Schumacher.

At the time, Gus was a stand-in and stunt dog for Heinrich, the star of the NBC children's television series, *Run, Joe, Run* (1974–1976), the story of an escaped military police dog being hunted by society. Since Schumacher didn't know if the series would be renewed for a second season, he auditioned Gus to play Won Ton Ton, and the dog won the role. So in a case of life imitating art, Gus, the unknown dog understudy, had a chance to become a big-screen movie star.

Trainer Karl Lewis Miller, who had trained Gus for his understudy television role, prepared him for the film as well. According to Miller, "The challenge of *Won Ton Ton* was that they wrote every imaginable, impossible gag for that dog to do. The problem with that was that now we had to take that dog and really condition him to be an athletic, working dog." Miller had twelve weeks preparation time to perform the seemingly impossible, and he did. His success was due not only to his skill as a trainer but to Gus's personality. "That dog had so much heart and just wanted to please us," Miller remembered.

In addition to Gus's screen personality and animal action, the novelty of the film resulted from the cameo appearances of more than 70 Hollywood stars, including Morey

Amsterdam, Billy Barty, Broderick Crawford, Rhonda Fleming, Zsa Zsa Gabor, Dorothy Lamour, Ethel Merman, Henny Youngman, and Johnny Weissmuller. Gus won a PATSY Award in 1977 for his work in *Won Ton Ton*.

After *Won Ton Ton*, Gus did major pieces of action in many Hollywood films but was never a lead dog again. According to Miller, "Gus was like Jack Elam, the famous character actor. He's been in everything, but you just can't remember his name."

"On, King! On, You Huskies!"

The magnificent Yukon King and Sergeant Preston (Richard Simmons).

From 1947 to 1955, snow swirled and relentless North winds whipped through radios tuned to the ABC program, *The Challenge of the Yukon*. Listeners eagerly awaited the further adventures of Sergeant William Preston of the Northwest Canadian Mounted Police and his malamute dog, Yukon King. Several radio actors played the role of Sergeant Preston—Paul Sutton had the role the longest—and the role of Yukon King was played not by a dog but by a man. Real dogs were used for the background sounds of the sled team, but all of Yukon King's "dialogue" was provided by Ted Johnstone. Charles Livingstone, who produced the radio series, said: "Ted was terrific! He could do any dog sound so you'd swear it was the real thing!"

From 1955 to 1958, Yukon King and Sergeant Preston made a successful transition to television and mushed their way through 78 half-hour color episodes of *Sergeant Preston of the Yukon*. Although set in Canada's Yukon, location shooting for the episodes took place in Aspen, Colorado, and Big Bear Lake and Hollywood, California. The episodes related the adventures of the Mountie, played by Richard Simmons; his horse Rex; and his team of huskies, led by the giant malamute, Yukon King, as they maintained law and order in the early days of the 1890s Gold Rush.

Working with one dog is a challenge; when a whole team of dogs is thrown into the mix, it makes for interesting experiences. At the time the series was in production, Richard Simmons told a reporter: "A harnessed team is a quivering mass of supercharged energy. But they're trained not to move until they receive a verbal command. Consequently, 'All Right,' 'Ready,' 'Let's go,' or 'Action' is forbidden language when working around the dogs. If you make a slip, they're off like rockets."

To avoid a premature launch, Yukon King's trainer, Beverly Allen and the other dog handlers developed a numeric code. "When everything is ready for the sleds to move, we use the number thirteen," Simmons said at the time. "We use this number because in the years these dogs have been trained as a team, they've learned all the numbers through twelve, which were used earlier as ready signals. I never thought I would have to brush up my arithmetic to keep one step ahead of a pack of dogs."

Charles Livingstone, who directed several episodes of *Sergeant Preston of the Yukon*, had his own set of difficulties. He recalled one episode that had a scene requiring Yukon King and the entire team of huskies to lie in the snow outside Sergeant Preston's cabin. This scene was shot on an interior studio set complete with cabin exteriors, trees, and fake snow. "All of a sudden, one after another of the dogs started to get sick," Livingstone said. "We watched them to see what was wrong and discovered that they were eating the white sand, thinking it was snow—the sand that was supposed to look like snow on the studio set."

Controlling supercharged energy on a daily basis and occasionally eating fake snow takes a lot out of a dog. When the pressure of performing on the series became overwhelming, Yukon King laid down and refused to act. "He had more sense than a lot of people," Simmons said.

ZAMBA

The "Puurr-fect" Co-Star for Shirley Jones

Zamba approves of Tony Randall's cuisine in *Fluffy*. (*Archive Photos*)

The biggest cat that ever purred for animal-lover Shirley Jones was Zamba, her lion co-star in the 1965 film *Fluffy*. The film tells the story of a scientist, played by Tony Randall, who wants to prove that wild animals can become pets if they are trained properly. He domesticates a lion, Fluffy, and suffers repercussions when just the sight of a lion causes people to panic. Scientist and pet take refuge in a hotel, and Jones falls in love with both of them.

"Zamba and I became very good friends," Jones remembered. "He became like a house pet to me. He really got to know me, and when I would come on the set, he would always come to greet me, and he would lay his huge head right in my lap. He was adorable."

One scene required Jones to lie on the bed while Zamba strolled into the room and lay down beside her. Jones was supposed to see the lion, act terrified, and slide to the floor. Zamba had other ideas about how to play that scene.

"Zamba put his giant paw over my face and held me there," Jones said. "Fortunately, he was very gentle. It felt like a huge catcher's mitt. But as you can well imagine, everyone on the set was petrified. But as it turned out, Zamba really wasn't trying to hurt me; he was just playing around. He was really a darling."

Zamba's gentle, playful nature was the result of the affection training he received from the time he was a cub, according to his trainer Ralph Helfer. Helfer insisted that Zamba share sleeping quarters with him, eat in the kitchen during family meals, and wile away the evening hours in the trainer's company. Helfer also believed that Zamba's partial vegetarian diet diminished what normally would have been the aggressive nature of a carnivore.

Zamba's unique nature was tested when he won the role of King the lion in the 1962 film *The Lion*. Based on the novel *The Lion* by Joseph Kessel, the film relates the story of a young girl (Pamela Franklin) in Africa whose best friend is a lion she has loved since it was a cub, the Masai warrior (Paul Oduor) who loves the girl, and the battle the warrior and the lion wage for the girl's love. At the climactic scene, the warrior and the lion are engaged in mortal combat, and to save the young man's life, the girl's step-father (Trevor Howard) must shoot the lion.

For that scene, Helfer acted as the double for the actor playing the Masai warrior. Helfer gave 500-pound Zamba the cue to attack. "He hit me like a ton of rocks, and his great front legs and paws gathered me up like a toy," Helfer remembered. "His mane choked my breath. For a split second I was allowed to roll out from under him, but he attacked again and again, until his great weight held me to the ground." The next thing Helfer knew was that Zamba's eyes had narrowed, his mouth opened, and his fangs locked around Helfer's arm—gently, ever so gently. As the scene continued, the girl's father raised his gun and "shot" King. The capsules of movie blood hidden in his mane broke, the red liquid ran, the girl cradled the lion in her lap, and he "died." After the cameras stopped rolling, Helfer got up and went to check on Zamba.

"One great amber eye opened, and a forepaw shot up and caught me around the neck," he said. "He pulled me to him, and with his big, raspy tongue, he began licking my face."

Zamba was honored for his amazing performance. In 1963, Zamba received a PATSY Award.

In addition to his film work, Zamba was also recognized for his work in commercials. In 1968, Zamba won a PATSY Award for his role as the lion in the Dreyfus Fund ads.

EPILOGUE

In the glitzy world of motion pictures and television, most animal actors don't "horse" around. They have a job to do, food and affection rewards to claim, so they get down to business. Whether they have a "whale" of a part or a role that's just "bear"ly on the screen, animal actors and their trainers "dog"gedly pursue perfection in practicing their craft. Such tenacity frequently "cat"apults animal actors into the realm of animal stars. And we love them for the smiles, the tears, and the joy they bring us. Here's to our amazing animal actors and their talented trainers—you're the greatest! (And I'm not "lion.")

Bibliography

The author wishes to acknowledge the following sources, which were invaluable during the writing of *Amazing Animal Actors*.

Andrews, Bart. *Lucy & Ricky & Fred & Ethel: The Story of I LOVE LUCY*. New York: EP Dutton & Co., Inc., 1976.

Autry, Gene, and Mickey Herskowitz. *Back in the Saddle Again*. Garden City, New York: Doubleday & Company, Inc., 1978.

Berg, A. Scott. *Goldwyn: A Biography*. New York: Alfred A. Knopf, Inc., 1989.

Bond, Tommy "Butch," and Ron Genini. *Darn Right It's Butch: Memories of Our Gang*. Wayne, Pennsylvania: Morgin Press, Inc., 1994.

Brooks, Tim, and Earle Marsh. *The Complete Directory to Prime Time Network TV Shows 1946–Present*. New York: Ballantine Books, 1979.

Cannon, Lou. *Reagan*. New York: G. P. Putnam's Sons, 1982.

Cooper, Jackie, and Dick Kleiner. *Please Don't Shoot My Dog: The Autobiography of Jackie Cooper*. New York: William Morrow & Co., 1981.

Dietz, Howard. *Dancing in the Dark*. New York: Quadrangle/The New York Times Book Co., 1974.

Edelson, Edward. *Great Animals of the Movies*. Garden City, New York: Doubleday, 1980.

Essoe, Gabe. *Tarzan of the Movies*. New York: Citadel Press, Inc., 1968.

Francisco, Charles. *Gentleman: The William Powell Story*. New York: St. Martin's Press, 1985.

Frank, Gerold. *Judy*. New York: Harper & Row, Publishers, 1975.

Green, Joey. *The GET SMART Handbook*. New York: Collier Books, 1993.

Hammett, Dashiell. *The Novels of Dashiell Hammett*. New York: Alfred A. Knopf, 1965.

Harmetz, Aljean. *The Making of The Wizard of Oz*. New York: Dell Publishing, 1989.

Hay, Peter. *MGM: When the Lion Roars*. Atlanta, Georgia: Turner Publishing, Inc., 1991.

Helfer, Ralph. *The Beauty of the Beasts: Tales of Hollywood's Wild Animal Stars*. Los Angeles: Jeremy P. Tarcher, Inc., 1990.

Heymann, C. David. *Liz: An Intimate Biography of Elizabeth Taylor*. New York: Carol Publishing Group, 1995.

Higham, Charles. *Merchant of Dreams: Louis B. Mayer, M.G.M. and the Secret Hollywood*. New York: Donald I. Fine, Inc., 1993.

Javna, John. *Animal Superstars*. Milwaukee: Hal Leonard Books, 1986.

——. *Cult TV: A Viewer's Guide to the Shows America Can't Live Without*. New York: St. Martin's Press, 1985.

Kelley, Kitty. *Elizabeth Taylor: The Last Star*. New York: Simon & Schuster, 1981.

Koehler, William R. *The Wonderful World of Disney Animals*. New York: Howell Book House, Inc., 1979.

Kotsilibas-Davis, James, and Myrna Loy. *Myrna Loy: Being and Becoming*. New York: Alfred A. Knopf, 1987.

Leder, Jane Mersky. *Stunt Dogs*. Mankato, Minnesota: Crestwood House, 1985.

Maddox, Brenda. *Who's Afraid of Elizabeth Taylor?* Philadelphia: M. Evans and Company, Inc., 1977.

Maltin, Leonard, and Richard W. Bann. *The Little Rascals: The Life and Times of Our Gang.* New York: Crown Publishers, Inc., 1977, 1992.

Matthews, Charles. *Oscar A to Z: A Complete Guide to More Than 2,400 Movies Nominated for Academy Awards.* New York: Doubleday, 1995.

McCrohan, Donna. *The Life and Times of Maxwell Smart.* New York: St. Martin's Press, 1988.

Moore, Dick. *Twinkle, Twinkle, Little Star.* New York: Harper & Row, Publishers, 1984.

Morella, Joe, and Edward Z. Epstein. *Judy: The Films and Career of Judy Garland.* New York: The Citadel Press, 1969.

Morris, Georgia, and Mark Pollard. *Roy Rogers: King of the Cowboys.* San Francisco: HarperCollins Publishers, 1994.

Nalven, Nancy. *The Famous Mister Ed: The Unbridled Truth about America's Favorite Talking Horse.* New York: Warner Books, 1991.

Nash, Jay Robert, and Stanley Ralph Ross. *The Motion Picture Guide.* Chicago: Cinebooks, 1987.

Paietta, Ann C., and Jean L. Kauppila. *Animals on Screen and Radio: An Annotated Sourcebook.* Metuchen, New Jersey: The Scarecrow Press, Inc., 1994.

Peary, Danny. *Cult Movies: The Classics, the Sleepers, the Weird and the Wonderful.* New York: Dell Publishing, Co., 1981.

Pitts, Michael R. *Famous Movie Detectives.* Metuchen, New Jersey: The Scarecrow Press, 1979.

Quirk, Lawrence J. *The Complete Films of William Powell.* Secaucus, New York: The Citadel Press, 1986.

Reagan, Ronald, and Richard G. Hubler. *Where's the Rest of Me?: The Ronald Reagan Story.* New York: Duell, Sloan and Pearce, 1965.

Rogers, Roy, and Dale Evans with Jane Stern and Michael Stern. *Happy Trails: Our Life Story.* New York: Simon & Schuster, 1994.

Rothel, David. *The Great Show Business Animals.* San Diego: A.S. Barnes & Company, Inc., 1980.

——. *Who Was That Masked Man?* San Diego: A.S. Barnes & Company, 1981.

Shipman, David. *Judy Garland: The Secret Life of an American Legend.* New York: Hyperion, 1993.

Spoto, Donald. *The Biography of Elizabeth Taylor.* New York: HarperCollins, 1995.

Stowers, Carlton. *Happy Trails: The Story of Roy Rogers and Dale Evans.* Waco, Texas: Word Books, 1979.

Taylor, Elizabeth. *Elizabeth Taylor: An Informal Memoir.* New York: Harper & Row, Publishers, 1964.

Terrace, Vincent. *Encyclopedia of Television Series, Pilots, and Specials 1937–1973.* New York: New York Zoetrope, 1986.

Walker, Alexander. *The Life of Elizabeth Taylor.* New York: Grove Weidenfeld, 1991.

Weatherwax, Rudd B., and John H. Rothwell. *The Story of Lassie: His Discovery & Training from Puppyhood to Stardom.* New York: Duell, Sloan & Pearce, 1950.

Williams, Barry, and Chris Kreski. *Growing Up Brady: I Was a Teenage Greg.* New York: HarperCollins, 1992.